THE VIRGIN OF PRINCE STREET

AMERICAN LIVES

Series editor: Tobias Wolff

THE **VIRGIN** OF **PRINCE STREET**

EXPEDITIONS *into* DEVOTION

SONJA LIVINGSTON

University of Nebraska Press | Lincoln

Acknowledgments for the use of
copyrighted material appear on
page 162, which constitutes
an extension of the copyright page.

This is a work of literary nonfiction.
Some names have been changed to
respect those who may not wish to be
identified. For consistency and clarity
Corpus Christi is used as the name
of the Rochester, New York, parish,
though it became known as Our Lady
of the Americas in 2007 and part of St.
Frances Xavier Cabrini Parish in 2011.

Library of Congress
Cataloging-in-Publication Data
Names: Livingston, Sonja, author.
Title: The virgin of Prince Street: expedi-
tions into devotion / Sonja Livingston.
Description: Lincoln: University of
Nebraska Press, [2019] | Series: American
lives | Includes bibliographical references.
Identifiers: LCCN 2019005281
ISBN 9781496217172 (pbk.: alk. paper)
ISBN 9781496218568 (epub)
ISBN 9781496218575 (mobi)
ISBN 9781496218582 (pdf)
Subjects: LCSH: Livingston, Sonja. | Spiri-
tual life – Catholic Church. | Devotion. |
Christian pilgrims and pilgrimages. |
Catholics – Biography.
Classification: LCC BX4705.L6625 A3 2019
LC record available at
https://lccn.loc.gov/2019005281

Set in Malabar LT Pro by E. Cuddy.
Designed by L. Auten.

For

Father Bob Werth
who won't like the attention of a dedication
but whose own dedication could fill a thousand books

&

Father Jim Callan
who gathered us close to the table
and showed what Corpus Christi could be

CONTENTS

AUTHOR'S NOTE

In 1963 Jesuit theologian Hugo Rahner described the Roman Catholic Church as a "tired, dusty pilgrimess" in the desert. If she was weary back in 1963, she's in need of smelling salts today. Vocations continue to dwindle. Church closings persist. Ongoing scandals have disheartened even the most stalwart Catholics, with tradition fading or become increasingly politicized. Perhaps it's no surprise that in the United States Roman Catholicism is losing numbers faster than any other denomination. Even those who consider themselves Catholic – via active attendance or cultural affiliation – overwhelmingly disagree with aspects of Church teaching, especially on matters of human sexuality and gender. Despite a tremendously popular pope, the Church seems caught up in a cloud of two-thousand-year-old incense smoke.

Imagine my astonishment then, when, a few years ago, I found myself at my childhood church. I looked around one Sunday morning, mystified. The rows of empty pews did not baffle me, nor did the worn fixtures or the precariousness of Corpus Christi's survival. I was surprised only by how much I cared. My attempt to make sense of this lingering connection – the various curiosities and anxieties it unleashed – led to the journeys that follow. While the expeditions didn't fully rehabilitate me as a Catholic, they opened me to something I'd been missing. When the norm is walking away, devotion itself becomes a radical proposition. Deliberately embracing one thing – no matter how troubled – caused my appreciation for all things to grow. Such openness cannot be contained. What began as a series of essayistic explorations became acts of reclamation. I too am a dusty pilgrimess, it turns out, who found herself fed by the fruit of abandoned gardens and the swell of underground streams.

THE VIRGIN OF PRINCE STREET

SEARCH FOR THE VIRGIN, PART I

Rochester

It's impossible to say when the Virgin took leave of Corpus Christi Church.

I did not see the perfect blue of her cloak when I returned a few Christmases ago, but a blizzard of statues had descended that year and she may have been hidden among them. Plaster saints did not outnumber parishioners, but neither were they far behind. A half dozen Marys occupied the sanctuary and just as many Blessed Spouses. One Saint Joseph looked down from the organ loft while another kept company with the Gospel writers in the narthex. Jesus appeared as the Sacred Heart, the Risen Christ, in his passion on the cross, and as a baby in his mother's arms. Anthony of Padua loomed large, as did Thérèse of Lisieux, Martin de Porres, the two Francises (Xavier and Assisi) – and did I only imagine Saint Lucy with her platter of eyes?

I'd convinced my husband to take a detour after a candlelight vigil at his parents' Presbyterian church. The simple elegance of the service had been a good match for my head, but the tangled mess of my heart longed for something else.

"I need a statue of a saint," I joked, but we both understood that a statue was shorthand for many things – differences in religious backgrounds, for instance, as well as a certain willingness to deviate from logic where devotion is concerned. "Let's stop at Corpus Christi on the way home."

I'd loved the sandstone building on East Main and Prince Streets for as long and as hard as I've ever loved anything. With its high-flung ceiling and gothic arches, the church was the most beautiful place I knew. And I was more beautiful in it. Not physically – though a mirror in the basement did, in fact, soften my features; I only mean that I was a better version of myself at Corpus Christi. Everyone was.

But as much as the parish was part of my life, I was never traditionally religious. This would have been impossible given my mother's Catholicism, which veered wildly over the years. My father, who hailed from a more traditional Catholic family, was a stranger to me. There was only my mother wearing a scapular and dragging all seven of her children to re-enact the stations of the cross on city streets on Good Friday, or sleeping in on Sundays and missing Mass for years at a time. Further complicating this legacy was the fact that ours was an unusually progressive parish, allowing altar girls, for instance, decades before they were permitted by Rome. There was no fire or brimstone. No excessive talk of sin and redemption. Just folk Masses with Cat Stevens songs and youth retreats where we talked about social justice and made self-esteem collages. A solid foundation – exactly what I needed, in fact – but not exactly typical.

Perhaps more than any other factor, my own skepticism thwarted any hope of theological convention. A dreamy child by nature, I was anchored firmly to earth by the vigorous brand of realism that unpredictable living conditions often impart. Faith was a luxury, it seemed to me, and God a pipe dream – a heavenly Father for girls with picture-perfect families, shiny lunchboxes, and dispositions far more cheerful than my own. So, while I came eagerly to Mass, served proudly at the altar, and noticed the way that people from the neighborhood perked up at church like wilted plants given doses of water and light, I was not – by even the most generous interpretation of the word – devout.

Devout. Past participle of the root word for devotion, kissing cousin to devoted and the more glamorous-sounding devotee – the word always seemed equal parts old-fashioned and feverish to me. Like the grandma who came to church wearing a black veil and clutching her rosary and swooned so hard during the Our Father she fell over like clockwork. I was not the swooning type – nor was I ever likely to be – but fast-forward a few decades and there I was on Christmas Eve, stuffed with a sensible sermon and elegant hymns but hungry for something else.

My husband and I arrived at the tail end of Mass, slipping into a pew and laughing at our terrible planning – how late we were and at a Spanish service, no less. But we fitted ourselves into the back of the church, which was empty and dark compared to the front where the small congregation was clustered. That's when we noticed the statues. Reigning from pedestals and swooping from corners, the life-sized figures cast exaggerated shadows in the half-light. That we'd just come from an uncluttered Presbyterian sanctuary only heightened the sense of avalanche.

"There aren't usually this many." The defensive tone of my voice annoyed me. I'd wanted a statue, after all. And there we were, surrounded by more than I'd ever seen assembled in one place. "I don't know where they all came from."

"It's fine," he said, but shifted his weight to avoid the gaze of the black-cloaked Mother Cabrini standing sentry near the altar. He didn't have to distract himself for very long, however, because just then the choir started up and the church sprang to life as women in colorful skirts and men in guayaberas beat back winter with their maracas and palitos. We clapped along with guitar and tambourine, singing makeshift Spanish and becoming giddy as the old church filled with the emerald greens and salted blues of old San Juan.

The following Christmas the longing arose in me again. We arrived early, sat closer to the front, and waited for the choir to reawaken our sluggish hearts. But our planning did not pay off. The Mass was in English this time and featured an entirely different choir. The statuary had also largely subsided. It was as if a tremendous tidal wave had rolled into Corpus Christi and carried the legion of saints out to sea. Where had they all gone? I wondered. The church looked more as it had when I was young. It was this thought that led me to look to the right-side altar and to realize with sudden clarity that the blue-cloaked statue I'd grown up with was no longer there.

It's not as if the sanctuary lacked images of the Blessed Mother. Our Lady of Mt. Carmel inhabited the niche where my Mary once stood. Our Lady of Perpetual Help bloomed quietly in the left transept. A framed print of Our Lady of Guadalupe hung beside the lectern. Reassuring images. Beautiful images. Still, I continued to twist in my pew, scanning corners and alcoves for the one I knew best.

"Joy to the world," the choir sang, but the words did not touch me. I looked up and into the organ loft. Nothing. The Virgin of Prince Street had disappeared.

"Why do you look familiar?" the priest asked as he greeted us after Mass and I mumbled something about all my years at Corpus Christi.

"Where do you go now?"

"Nowhere," I sputtered, unsure of how to politely convey that I hadn't attended regularly in twenty years – not since I'd left this very church, in fact.

"I live in Memphis half the year," I offered, as if there were no Catholic church in the entire state of Tennessee. And before he had a chance to try to untangle my murky geographic and religious status, I asked what happened to the Blessed Mother. Not the best small talk to a priest on Christmas Eve, perhaps, but I could not let it be.

"What?" He squinted and bent in, as if he hadn't quite heard.

"The old statue of the Virgin." I nodded toward the altar. "Where is she?"

When he realized I was asking about a statue, the priest looked suddenly weary and muttered something about not knowing while backing away from the pew.

I could not know he'd recently been embroiled over a statue.

When I returned to church later that year my new friend, Mary Engels, told me about her crusade on behalf of Saint Joseph. As Corpus Christi merged with other parishes – increasingly common as Rochester's Catholic churches continued to close – parishioners from Mt. Carmel and Holy Redeemer brought their hymns and traditions with them. But they also brought their statues, Mary explained, so that Corpus Christi's interior became more crowded with the influx of each new group. Longtime parishioners might grumble, but how could they really complain when they still had access to the church in which their parents had married and they'd had their children baptized?

This must have been the thinking when the Corpus Christi Joseph was removed from his altar and replaced with Mother Cabrini, patron of the newly clustered parish. The statue of Joseph landed in the basement, and this my new friend Mary could not abide. She bore Mother Cabrini no ill will – and, really, who could? – but Joseph's demotion rankled her and she, who is not given to timidity, made her feelings known.

"Joseph belongs on that altar," she told the priest, who'd only recently found himself assigned to the poorest cluster of churches in the diocese and would have had more than statues on his mind. But Mary kept at him. When her initial protestations were met with comments about the trickiness of such matters, she heightened her offensive.

"It's my dying wish," she said, "that Saint Joseph be returned."

Mary was in her nineties by then and talk of dying wishes no small thing. The priest pointed out the various sensitivities involved and reminded her of the abundance of statues, the distribution of which was out of his hands. But one Sunday before Mass he passed Mary's pew and asked if she noticed anything different today. She craned her neck left and, hallelujah, there he was. Outfitted with his carpenter's square and staff of lilies, good old Saint Joseph looked like he'd never left the niche where he'd stood for nearly a hundred years.

I knew I lacked the personality and the perseverance to persuade the priest to reinstate the original Virgin, and slowly realized that I lacked credibility too. Sure, I'd been baptized at Corpus Christi – and, in fact, had received all my sacraments there, making it the most stable spoke in the whirling wheel of my early life – but, whereas Mary Engels had started attending when FDR was president, I'd only recently ambled back, and, even then, just when I was in town. And though the priest was clearly kind – returning a statue when he had a hundred more pressing matters to attend to – I swear he glanced warily in my direction sometimes, suspicious perhaps of my strange return or obvious statue fixation.

Still, the Joseph story stayed with me.

They were a pair, after all – Mary and Joseph. If the Blessed Spouse could be recalled from the basement and set once again onto his altar, wasn't there hope for the Virgin as well?

1

Absolute Mystery

I hear the word, of course.

I go to church some Sundays, play *Al Green's Greatest Gospel Hits* on repeat in my car, and have spent a good portion of recent years in or near the Bible Belt. Still, the word *God* has never quite fitted itself to my ears. When I'm called upon to say it I get all shifty-eyed and spastic. I smile hard and mutter other words – *spirit, goodness, love* – anything but the word *God*, which sits like a fistful of rubber bands in my mouth.

God Bless you, people say, and unless I've sneezed I'm at a loss.

My friend Mary just moved into a nursing home and showed me around when I visited – the cafeteria, the sunroom with wicker plant stands and floral-padded chairs, the chapel with statues of the Blessed Mother and Jesus flanking the altar. At ninety-six years old and adorned with more medals of the saints than I can count, Mary has been my ardent and unlikely guide – and the one person who doesn't seem stunned – as I've made my way back to church.

"Go up and say hello," she said to me while nodding to the statues. The chapel was small with nowhere to hide, and my attempt to change the subject did not work. "Go on up and touch them," Mary said. "Show them that you're here and you care."

Well, I was there and I did care, but setting my hands against their cool plaster robes embarrassed me somehow, made me feel exposed and inauthentic. Which is how I feel when I attempt to use the word *God*. Like I'm touching Our Lady's pink painted feet while my friend Mary nods and looks on.

This is not a major problem in and of itself. We have great freedom when it comes to language. If we don't like a word we generally don't have to use it. Writers can be especially persnickety about such matters and keep running tallies of objectionable words in their heads. For years I simply lumped *God* in with words like *cerulean* and *staccato* and moved on.

The trouble began when I returned to Corpus Christi. *What on earth am I doing?* I'd ask anyone who'd listen, but stumbled even as I tried to formulate the question. Clearly, I needed to explore language itself – How was I to delve into the matter when I couldn't even bring myself to use the word *God*?

Devout Jews do not utter the God of Israel's name. In conversation they say *Holy One*, or *HaShem* (literally, the Name), while *Adonai* (Lord) is substituted in prayer. Even in writing, the Name must be handled with great care. Hyphens are inserted (G-d), or the tetragrammaton (the four Hebrew letters transliterated as YHWH, which many Christians pronounce *Yahweh*).

But even among Christians there's an awareness of the limitations of language where God is concerned.

Saint Anselm said: *God is that, the greater than which cannot be conceived.*

Saint Augustine said: *If you comprehend it, it is not God.*

Theologian Karl Rahner preferred *Absolute Mystery* to the word God, saying: *God's silence, the eerie stillness, is filled by the Word without words, by Him who is above all names.*

It's possible my problem is cultural. I grew up among people who did not like to reveal our tenderness. We went to Mass, yes. We fell in love and exercised the soft tissue of our hearts as best as we could – but to leave ourselves so open as to enthusiastically believe? This was madness.

But that doesn't entirely explain it. I have, despite it all, a proclivity toward softness. I've learned to say words like *honey* and *sweetness*, to enjoy the sounds of them, and to mostly mean them.

The larger problem is that even as a child I never expected words to be even exchanges for the truth. It wasn't just *God*. Other words troubled me. *Salvation. Purgatory.* The word *Christianity* itself. Beyond their basic definitions, what did they really mean? That the world was wondrous I could almost let myself believe, but religious language seemed to trap wonder into cardboard boxes. I still remember the day I quizzed parishioners after Mass about virgin motherhood. People stuck to the official account no matter how I battered them with facts gleaned from the sex education unit in fifth grade.

"Do you really believe," I asked, "that Mary became pregnant without a man?"

No one admitted doubt. No one suggested different ways of knowing or contemplation of words like faith and skepticism – or even *virginity* itself. Instead they clung to the story's literal hinges. The next day they'd return to their factories and typewriters and bus driving seats and needed this day of rest, I suppose, and, even more so, the magnificence of virgin birth. I almost understood. But how disappointed I was to learn that, while we shared the same cache of words, we knew so little of each other. How alone I suddenly felt. Bad enough to be a kid from the family that got food baskets every Christmas – now it seemed I was the only one at Corpus Christi who adored the Blessed Mother whether her virginity was figurative or not.

My misgivings did not keep me from church. I went eagerly and as often as I could. I thrived on what I found there, even if I could not name it, so I learned to make do. For as far back as I can remember, whenever anyone said *God* I simply added an *o* in my head, converting it to the word *good*.

God is good, someone will say after an unexpected triumph or to praise an especially brilliant day, and it's the one time I can nod and smile and not feel false.

But the word *good* is not the word *god*. They appear to have entirely different origins. *Good* comes from the old English (gōd), is cousin to *gather* and *-gether*, and derives from the Proto-Germanic (gōdaz) and the Proto Indo-European (ghedh), which means *to unite, be associated, to suit,* or *to fit.*

No one agrees on the origin of the word *god*. Used as both a proper noun for the supreme being and more generally to designate a deity-at-large, *god*, according to some theories, is rooted in the Old English word from the Proto-Germanic (guthan) meaning *to invoke* or *to pour out.*

God is perhaps uttered most effortlessly as a secular exclamation. *God damn it*, a driver yells as his truck slides into a muddy ditch. *God no*, the husband says as the surgeon emerges from the operating room with a frozen look on his face. *My god*, the lover murmurs while grazing the inside of her lip with a tooth. *OMG*, the student says, and we all *LOL*.

The word *God* springs from the gut in such cases, bypassing our ordinary filters. It's the last sound we make as we move toward speechlessness, the drop-off point to the vast ocean where language has no jurisdiction.

What we feel most, the poet Jack Gilbert wrote, *has no name.*

In the meantime the word *God* falls millions of times a day from our collective mouths, though there's no agreement on what we're talking about. To some God is an omnipotent guardian with a heap of white curls riding shotgun in the clouds. To many he's a young man strung up and suffering open wounds beyond the city walls. To others she's the fog of early morning, the green breath of trees.

Do you believe in God?

The question used to come regularly at day camp and public school – along with its theological cousin: *Have you been saved?* Most kids in the neighborhood wore cheap sneakers and hailed from one-parent households so that, other than categories of ethnicity and race, religion was one of the few distinctions between us. *Do you believe in God?* Some kid would ask and I'd still be spinning my wheels, caught up in an inarticulate loop long after he'd moved on.

These are a young person's questions, perhaps. The topic is too thorny for adults. As a culture we've grown more cautious about such matters, and with good cause. When they come at all these days, such questions are lobbed by radio preachers, sidewalk prophets, or brochure-wielding strangers who arrive in pairs at the front door. We talk openly of love and sex, politics and personal aspirations, family trouble and addiction – but on this topic we are uncharacteristically shy. Or justifiably wary. Either way, I had not been asked what I believed for years. Which is why I was so shocked when the question came from an acquaintance who learned I'd returned to church.

Do you believe in God?

Her voice was cool and clean, as though she were asking if I'd like soup with my salad. It seemed a bold question, maybe even rude – though, in retrospect, an obvious one too. But an impossible question just the same.

The word *God* is broken shorthand, a one-syllable exchange that tricks us into thinking we understand something of each other and how we see the world. She may as well have asked if I believed in the scent of gardenias wafting around Richmond on August evenings, the slow groan of their petals, or the word *belief* itself.

God is closer to us than our bodies, according to the Qur'an, closer than the jugular vein.

So near we approach the place where words have no business. Or have important business if only we learn to use them in new ways.

Some words get closer than others. Verbs do better than nouns. Metaphor occasionally pulls back the curtain to reveal glimpses. But even then we are only children tossing pebbles at the sky.

Still, we humans broker the world in words, so what else can we do but try?

Every semester I share the quote attributed to Chekhov: *Don't tell me the moon is shining; show me the glint of light on broken glass.* I talk with my writing students about the necessity for concrete language. *No ideas but in things*, I quote William Carlos Williams, then ask them to translate a series of ideas (*beauty, greed, poverty*) into seeable, touchable things (*a black feather landed on snow, a two-timing ex-boyfriend, the woman begging on West Franklin Street*). I sometimes add *God* to the list because the word seems to me the ultimate abstraction. And yet isn't the work of the artist – whether she identifies as believer or atheist – to not only show the light on broken glass but to try and touch the source of luminosity itself? What an impossible and lovely proposition – to attempt to build bridges with words to the mysterious expanse where language cannot join us.

That name – my conception of Him, Teresa of Ávila wrote, *extended to me a hand that led to a place where even His divine name could not exist.*

"I believe in goodness," I eventually replied to the woman who'd asked me about God, and was waiting for a *yes* or *no* answer. I confessed my trick of adding an *o* to the word, and though I meant it, I heard only the clumsiness of my reply, how slippery I sounded, and – between question and answer – how little we'd actually managed to say.

I should have told her about the sheep sprawling on the Scottish isle of Iona. Surrounded by moss and stone and the blue of the sea, they sink into the grasses there – lambs, overgrown ewes, and a few lucky cows – any doubt they're cradled by the earth itself never once entering their woolly heads.

I should have told her about the old men in Seville. The way they sat beside each other in a café where anyone foolish enough to be caught in the midday heat had taken refuge. One sat in his wheelchair, the other in a dining chair. They leaned in so close their birdlike heads nearly touched. Outside, the sun blinded and scorched. Inside, the men ate ice cream. One lifted a spoon and brought it to his friend's mouth. The other looked up and opened wide. Their laughter filled the café. They glowed, those men, and radiated pure delight – one for the taste of ice cream, the other for the pleasure of sharing it.

I should have told her about the fireflies my husband led me to this summer. We hiked along a dark trail to get to a small clearing in the park. I imagined spiders as we walked, worried about twisting my ankle, grumbled about having to do without my phone and my flashlight, but kept on until we reached a spot where the darkness was broken by tiny bursts of light. Flashes erupted in the grass, in the low-hanging branches, and in the crowns of trees. Like Christmas and New Year's rolled into one. Like the Fourth of July and every birthday candle ever lit. But quieter, truer somehow. When my friend asked if I believed in God, I should have told her about that hollow filled with light – the way we stood and stared and did not speak.

2

The Heart Is a First-Class Relic

These are the things you cannot plan for:

That one day you'll return to Corpus Christi Church. That you'll find between the stoup of holy water and statue of the Risen Christ an advertisement for a trip to the shrines of Quebec. That you'll roll your eyes, make exaggerated noises of derision, then promptly send in your check. That you'll emerge months later from a bus parked along the *Chemin Frère André* in Montreal. That the driver will bend a long leg against the hull and settle in for a smoke while you and a pack of fellow pilgrims bypass a gift shop glinting with rosaries, head toward the basilica, through the votive chapel, and up the stairs, where you'll eventually come to rest before an enshrined human heart.

The convert is the first one to her knees. *From Southern Baptist*, she'd whispered on the bus, but did not stop talking about Mother Angelica and EWTN long enough for me to ask the reason for the change. Beside her at the kneeler a man with a red face crosses himself as a squeamish family scuttles past. Most look on with a mix of curiosity and reverent nonchalance. We're Catholics, after all, and there's some pressure to appear unflustered as we shoehorn ourselves around the large panel of glass. A bouquet of yellow roses lies before the display along with flowers from someone's garden – lilies of the valley and forget-me-nots.

I look into the reliquary and remember the time I paid a dollar to get into the sideshow at the state fair in Syracuse, the concoctions floating in jars, the lowered lights and musty air. The shame and thrill of the memory rises and flits away or is tempered by the fact of growing up with the Sacred Heart of Jesus hung on our living room wall. Years of looking into that print prepared me, as did the life-size crucifix hauled out for Good Friday Mass, the bloodied feet the old ladies lined up to kiss. Now all these years later, I look through a panel of glass reinforced with iron lattice and flanked by a pair of brass doors onto which words have been engraved:

Ici repose dans la paix de Dieu le cœur du frère André.
Here rests in the peace of God the heart of Brother André.

If my husband had come to Montreal, this is where we'd have to part ways. *Gory*, he'd think but not say. *Primitive*. And I'd have to agree with him here. A human heart floating in formaldehyde *is* gruesome. Bowing before it *does* seem primitive. Why then does my body lock in place as I run my eyes over the slick bends of Brother André's heart?

My tour group has moved on. The last streamers of English are swallowed by French and Hindi as other groups wind past, but I do not join them.

I am, in most things, a thoughtful person, an admirer of southern trees and leggy shorebirds, a lover of wide rivers and singsong Irish novels. I'm prone to bouts of anger and flights of fancy and have never quite figured out my iPhone but am otherwise rational – an occasionally late but dependable payer of parking tickets and taxes; a woman who submits to annual physicals and frequent doses of oatmeal to manage her cholesterol; a teacher given more easily to skepticism than faith. How to explain, then, the way I wedge myself between women clicking their rosaries and lean in for a better look? Add it to the pile of cryptic instincts I've indulged over the past few months.

Such are my thoughts as my body comes undone from the tether of its head and lowers itself onto the kneeler before Brother André's long-dead heart.

Biology sees the organ before me as a muscle designed to circulate blood through the human body. Engineering calls it a highly efficient pump. Physics focuses on the pacemaker cells that generate electrical activity, the relaxation and contraction of valves, their assorted echoes and pulses. Chemistry might isolate the elements, noting oxygen and carbon and traces of copper and tin. Anatomy describes the organ as a hollow compartment divided into four chambers residing in the chest. Medicine encourages the consumption of leafy greens and daily walks, reminding us that diseases of the heart account for the majority of human deaths.

To the pilgrims at St. Joseph's Oratory the heart is a sacred object, the relic of a recently canonized saint. Relics have been used by humans for as long as we've bothered recording such matters and certainly long before. After his death the Buddha's body was divided and enshrined. A footprint of the prophet Muhammad, his sandals – even the hairs of his beard – have been preserved for centuries in Istanbul. But no tradition is more associated with relics than Roman Catholicism, whose followers venerate bits of wood and bone and cloth too numerous to count: the blood of Saint Valentine; a thin ribbon decorated with olive buttons believed to be the belt of the Blessed Virgin; links from Saint Peter's chains; splinters of Mary Magdalene's arm; slivers from the True Cross; a piece of Joseph's mantle; a thorn from Jesus's crown. Saint Anthony's tongue is venerated in Padua; his tooth is revered in Pittsburgh. The bones of Saint Thérèse of Lisieux have traveled the world – even into space aboard the space shuttle *Discovery*.

I was ten or so when a parishioner told me about the relic in our church. He brought me to the altar and pulled back the white cloth. There it was – embedded in an ivory-colored circle the size of a Communion wafer and set into the wood. "What is it?" I asked, uncertain whether the circle was marble or bone. And though I was the sort of kid who couldn't eat her Shake 'n Bake drumstick because there was no hiding the fact it had once been a leg, I brought my hand to the altar and ran a finger over its slick surface.

Relics make more sense when you consider Christianity's history and the persecution of its followers. Forced into catacombs for worship, early Christians gathered over their martyrs' remains to celebrate Mass. Martyrs were plentiful, as were the years of hiding, and people grew used to the sight of bones.

The Catholic Church divides relics into three classes: first-class relics are the physical remains of a saint or any object directly associated with the life of Jesus; second-class relics come from a saint's life, something they touched and made use of, such as a robe, a rosary, or book; a third-class relic results from a devotional object coming into intentional contact with a first- or second-class relic, such as a bit of cloth or medal touched by the remains of a saint. The heart, then, is a first-class relic.

Brother André's is not the only heart relic. Teresa of Ávila's is kept in a convent in Alba de Tormes. The heart of Saint Clare of Montefalco, which is said to contain a tiny crucifix, is kept on display in Umbria. Saint Jane de Chantal's rests in southeastern France. The hearts of twenty-five popes reside in the Church of Santi Vincenzo e Anastasio Trevi in Rome. In the last year alone the hearts of Saint Philip Neri, Saint John Vianney, Padre Pio, and Saint John Berchmans went on tour throughout the United States.

But Brother André's heart is special. In frail health and orphaned at the age of twelve, André Bessette was initially rejected by the Congregation of the Holy Cross in Montreal. When he was eventually accepted, it was in the lowly position of porter. André was devoted to Saint Joseph, a quiet saint and humble worker like himself. Brother André ministered to the sick and the poor, burning oil before a statue of Saint Joseph before rubbing it onto twisted legs and atrophied muscles. Whether it was the oil or the rarity of being touched, people said they were healed. Word of André's generosity spread, making him an icon in Montreal and, in 2010, a saint of the Catholic Church. In parts of Quebec people still describe an especially good person as having *un grand cœur du frère André* – a heart as big as Brother André's.

Brother André's heart was stolen back in March 1973. Thieves picked all three locks and removed the case from its pedestal. Later someone called the *Journal de Montreal* threatening to destroy the relic unless he was given $50,000. The voice led investigators to a parked car with a roll of film containing photos of the relic, though it was unclear how serious the demand for ransom was, and, in any event, the Archbishop of Montreal refused, saying: "Brother André's heart is priceless, so we refuse to pay any price for it."

Because the ransom was refused, the oratory learned to do without its prized relic and the thieves were left with an unclaimed heart on their hands. A year and a half later an anonymous phone call led to its discovery in the basement of an apartment building a few days before Christmas. Found in a locker, the relic was in good condition, though some of the formaldehyde had leaked. The Oratory's rector was thrilled to have it back: "It's a magnificent Christmas present for those who, since nearly half a century, have shown their faith for these sacred remains, as well as for us who are the designated keepers of Brother André's heart."

A happy ending for the shrine, but what becomes of a heart locked in a basement, leaking and double-boxed? What does it mean to be its designated keeper? And might the wayward relic actually belong to someone other than Brother André – another monk, perhaps – one who could not control his sweet tooth, whose thickened arteries sputtered and stopped as he stole a bite of *pouding chômeur* one frozen morning before prayer? Would it matter? At this point, what relationship does the organ bear to the body in which it stopped beating on the Feast of the Epiphany back in January 1937?

My husband prefers not to talk about the heart. More than anyone, Jim has encouraged me to accept my return to church, to follow wherever it leads, including to a shrine in Montreal. But now he winces and waves a hand as if to bat the subject away.

I've just arrived home after a day of travel delays and am in no mood to have my subject off-limits. Besides, he's just told me about someone who fell into a hot spring out west, a man whose body had vaporized and become immediate smoke.

"You just told a grisly story," I say. "And I can't even *talk*?"

"You can talk," he says. "Just not about internal organs."

We're both overly sensitive types. We curtail our trips to the lakeshore to look for sea ducks once hunting season begins. Neither of us can stand the pop of the hunters' guns or the sight of boats laden with mallards and long-tails. Neither has seen *The Texas Chainsaw Massacre*. Neither ever will. There's at least one mouse in our house we cannot bear to trap. But this is different. I look out the window for a minute, then turn back.

"What's the matter with the body – what's so wrong with talking about the human heart?" Exhaustion lends a soap opera quality to my voice, making the moment into melodrama, when what I mean to say is that, of all the people in the world, I would most like to talk with him about the heart.

The savviest of Catholics would explain that, despite the kneeler and pedestal and flowers, Brother André's heart is not being worshipped. The relic merely provides a physical connection to a holy person while serving as a reminder of his humanity and our own capacity for goodness. But those who come by the millions before the heart may not require such distinctions. To them the relic provides access to a man who, having healed in life, might do the same in death – and the closer the saint to the life of Jesus, the more likely the saint's ability to intervene on behalf of seekers. Pilgrims at the nearby shrine at Beaupré, for instance, are buoyed not only by the presence of Saint Anne's relics but by her status as Mary's mother and Jesus's grandmother. Who could deny their grandmother anything? they ask while swapping stories of mended ankles and cured knees. Such pilgrims parade before Brother André's heart, fixing their eyes upon another sign:

> *Prière pour obtenir une faveur spéciale par intercession de saint frère André.*
> Pray to obtain a special request at the intercession of Brother André.

A few years ago, archeologists discovered five embalmed hearts among the ruins of a convent in Rennes. Heart burial was not uncommon among nobles in medieval Europe. The fourteenth-century warrior-king Robert the Bruce famously requested that Sir James Douglas carry his heart on a crusade. With his friend's heart in a silver box, James sailed to Spain by way of Compostela and, when he died in battle in 1332, both his body and Bruce's heart were sent back to Scotland.

Only one of the five hearts at Rennes belonged to a woman, and this was degraded beyond repair. To the scientists' delight, the others were preserved enough to lend themselves to CT scans and MRIs. One belonged to Toussaint de Perrien, knight of Brefeillac, whose death in August 1649 did not stop his wife from tending his heart. Louise saw to it that the organ was washed with lavender, sealed with beeswax, and placed in a silver urn. When she died seven years later, Louise's body was outfitted in a cape and wool dress, leather shoes with cork soles, and a scapular around her right arm. Her hands held not only a crucifix but the urn containing her husband's heart. There it remained for four hundred years, as the world launched forward; religion loosened its grip as Linnaeus organized the world into a system of charts and graphs, Darwin took notes on South American mockingbirds, and Mendel looked so closely at pea plants that entire worlds opened before his eyes. Above ground: Telescopes. Street lamps. Crumbling monastery walls. Van Leeuwenhoek, Curie, and Einstein. La Salle following a muddy river in the New World and claiming Louisiana for France. Pope Pius VI overthrown by Napoleon. Men on the moon. The chant of nuns moving from cloisters to spinning silver discs. All of this – war and plague and new sources of light – while beneath the earth Louise held tight to Toussaint's heart.

I was a child, five or six years old and trapped by the babysitter's sons, when I had my first look inside the body. They lived on a farm, this family, which numbed them to the act of killing, and once, finding me especially weak, one of the teenaged boys hooked me from behind and made me watch as the other gutted the rabbit they'd shot. Probably they'd carted the rabbit home from the woods like a prize and I'd tried to run. The sight of my softness, all pink belly and trembling lower lip, might have pained them as much as their loud boots and hunting rifles pained me. So, they held me there as they set the rabbit on the table, and with a clean cut opened it up, as if the knife were a zipper and the rabbit a purse. I struggled and cried and squeezed my eyes shut – but was unable to avoid seeing liver and lung slip from the body's clutch.

It was horrible, I thought for many years, and those boys beyond redemption. But there was something else, I understood even then – something about witnessing the body unfolding from its lair, and all that's held under the skin. Our unseen parts. How quickly they stopped beating. How easily they fell out.

My friend Mary is the most openly devout person I know. She keeps a crucifix blessed by Padre Pio in her change purse and lifts it like gold to let people pray from it, while watching to be sure it's returned. Reports of miracles swarm forever from her mouth. Religious statues rise from every surface of her house. The Blessed Mother, of course, but Joseph too, and in one room alone two Infants of Prague. Such unconcealed devotion usually embarrasses me, but Mary's so enthusiastic in her approach to everything in life that with her I do not flinch. I even agree to pray from her Padre Pio cross once, though I slip into another room to spare her the discomfort on my face.

When Mary's beau asked her to marry him back in the 1950s, she told him she was flattered but would have to check with Saint Joseph before she could say for sure.

"What?" he said. "I ask you to marry me and you have to run it by Saint Joseph?"

Yes, she said, and traveled three hundred miles north to the Oratory in Montreal, the one founded by Brother André, the very same place where his heart is displayed. Mary would have walked through the votive chapel, past walls covered with canes left by those who'd reported healings – all that wood and the heat of ten thousand candles lending the scent of sawdust to the air. She'd have stopped to light a candle before moving on to Brother André's tomb, but only after ascending the steps of the oratory on her knees the way some pilgrims do. She said yes to George all those years ago, she tells me, because by the time she made it to the top Saint Joseph's answer had come to her loud and clear.

"So what do you think of that?" Mary asks, eyebrow raised.

"A miracle," she says before I have time to answer.

I consider the various reasons we find to say yes or no to each other, and, if yes, how often we must say it beyond the first time, how cumbersome it can become, that one word, again and again, like climbing a stair at a time toward the dome of the largest church in Canada. But Mary has no time for such internal dawdling and grabs my hand for confirmation.

"A miracle," I say. "Yes."

The heart is a messy business. We accuse some people of wearing them on their sleeves, but this is only metaphor. The heart is, by definition, the inmost portion of the self. The closest we come to showing it is in the company of a new love, when one need only set ear to chest to follow the swift percussion of blood. But such clamor passes quickly and for most of our days the heart is contained in its quiet cage. I can see why my husband wishes to avoid the chaos of the opened body – why Brother André's heart might seem to him the same as the pile of ducks in the hunters' boats. The animal gone slack, the ribboned muscle heavy and spent. Impossible to fathom that what once spun and vibrated can simply stop.

Maybe those boys did me a kindness all those years ago by showing me how slick our insides, how red and how tender. Perhaps the pilgrims at the oratory are not so misguided – or, if misguided, do not altogether waste their time.

We exist in a sea of hearts. Even when we do not speak of them, they're there. Big ones. Flabby ones. Old ones churning their way toward their final few pumps. New ones eager as spring birds. Rheumy fluttery valves. Constricted arteries. Barnacled veins. But no matter their quality or the characteristics of the people into whose bodies they're set – their particular habits, transgressions, and longings – the heart is electric. Science tells us this. Religion too. Here biologist and pilgrim lean in to examine the pink chambers and come away together, eyes wide in recognition.

That the heart will one day stop beating cannot diminish its perfection. That it is occasionally stolen, ransomed, or locked away – none of this changes its basic contours.

I would like to tell my husband about Brother André's heart – the way the case and setting are too ornate for its rough elegance; how the oratory, the reliquary, even the relic itself, are merely a shrine to something else. Something to do with the turning of cells and the deepest parts of ourselves laid open and fully regarded. Something related to Mary climbing those stairs, the pilgrims clicking their rosaries, the convent in France, and Louise touching Toussaint all those years underground. Something about the way we've learned to guard so well against fervor – and for a thousand good reasons, given the brutality that blind devotion often inspires. Still, I would like to ask him, whose opinions on the heart matter most, whether, in our steadfast allegiance to level-headedness, we've somehow lost sight of what lies within us and all that we might do.

SEARCH FOR THE VIRGIN, PART II

Rochester

For all my affection, it might seem as if the Prince Street Virgin were the loveliest lady in the world. In truth, my Mary was not grand.

Where other Virgins were topped by radiant diadems or crowned with halos of light, ours was outfitted with a meager veil and was similarly modest underfoot. She did not trample a serpent's head, for instance, nor stand upon a slip of gilded moon. She was not a woman of dramatic gestures. Her arms extended outward but only just so. Her white plaster robe was molded and fixed – no bend of knee or wayward foot caused the gown to ripple or pool. Nor did her mantle flap about her body in a sumptuous wave as did the mantles of other more riotous Virgins. Her expression was more pensive than sweet, her lips tinted the barest shade of pink. Model of humility. Queen of a working-class parish. The Corpus Christi Mary was as down to earth as one could be while being out of this world. Her sole extravagance was the garland of silk roses placed in her hands at some May crowning years before, but, by the time I made my First Communion, May crownings had become a thing of the past and the pink petals were faded and spent.

To me she was beautiful. I loved most of all the legion of blue glass candles flickering at her feet. As a child I'd once had a fit, hid from my mother, and was stuck in church after a vigil Mass. When I emerged from the room in which I'd been accidentally locked overnight, the Virgin's was the face

I looked to before running out the heavy wood doors down Main and Goodman Streets toward my own mother. Mary was the softest spot in the church – softer perhaps than anywhere at home.

Running from my mother and hiding overnight in a church are not as surprising as they might seem. I was abnormally skilled at making myself scarce. A French exit, some label such disappearing acts. An Irish good-bye. Call it what you will, it boils down to a sort of willful evaporation and is one of my truest gifts.

My mother claims I wandered away more than her other children, vanishing so often as a toddler she considered tethering me to the porch rails. I cultivated the capacity over the years. As a senior at East High I once left a classroom by inching my desk ever so slowly toward the door until only a foot or so remained, enough – as the teacher talked to someone near the back – to slide from the room and abandon my desk in the doorframe like a clunky old car.

The question then is not why I left Corpus Christi in my mid-twenties. Or why, when the priest could not explain the whereabouts of the Virgin on Christmas Eve, I slipped quietly out the door. The question is why I returned.

Returning to church at Christmas is not all that unusual. Christmas and Easter Catholics are so common they've inspired a list of monikers. Two-Timers, they're sometimes called. Chreasters. Poinsettia and Lily Catholics. CEOs (Christmas and Easter Only). A&Ps (Ashes & Palms). Cultural Catholics. The list goes on. But if I was a two-timer, how to explain my attendance the next time I was in Rochester? During my teaching breaks? Throughout a sabbatical the following year?

I visited other churches from time to time, but the draw was always Corpus Christi. The priest still seemed to regard me with suspicion sometimes but was obviously exceptional. There were two priests actually – one friendly and young, the other older and extravagantly offbeat. The latter, was, of course, the one to whom I attached myself.

But even the best priest can only do so much. He could not eliminate my discomfort with religious language or banish my uneasiness over problematic aspects of church teaching. If my return to church was some sort of spiritually centered midlife crisis, I wondered, why not head to a monastery in Nova Scotia or a Balinese oceanfront retreat? Or, if my heart insisted that I stay in the realm of Christianity, why not join the Quakers or the Unitarians whose doctrine and politics did not rile me? A place where I'd be surrounded by people who listened to public radio and be given a nametag and meaningful committee assignment instead of information on eucharistic adoration and Planned Parenthood protests? Wasn't waking early on Sunday mornings to attend the church on East Main and Prince Streets a giant step backward? Perhaps. But what appears to be a backward step is sometimes the only way forward, and the act of returning to anything was new to me.

If it's pain or chaos that sends us back to former sanctuaries – and, let's face it, it most often is – I had no specific source to explain my own. I'd experienced no sudden illness, singular trauma, or particular upheaval. I'd had my share of heart-ache, of course. I was leaving the safety of my midforties for the uncharted territory of my late forties, and the sorrow that had arrived with the realization I would not be a mother after years of trying showed no signs of lifting. Somewhere along the line, the polite but distant relationship I'd maintained for years with my own mother had fizzled out to just plain distant. My husband and I treasured each other but struggled in our marriage and wondered at times where things were headed.

But I also had my share of joy. A new crop of students arrived every semester, eager and brilliant, and I enjoyed some success in a career that seemed custom-made for my tendency toward creative introspection. That I was occasionally lonely seemed the price one paid for living in general and for the richness of solitude more specifically. I had friends whose company I cherished and who seemed to cherish me back. I took regular trips to new places, enjoyed a bevy of nieces and nephews, cared about my siblings – and even had a few I still talked to – no small feat in a troubled family. And while my husband and I continued to wrestle with things like forgiveness and compromise, we held hands sometimes and marveled over the rush of heart-shaped leaves cascading from catalpa trees. We stood on abandoned trails listening to the hollow call of bitterns among the cattails and walked in southern swamps, laughing as turtles plunked one at a time from overcrowded logs into murky streams. A good life, overall. A wondrous life, considering how tumultuously it had begun. Still and all, something was missing, and so my body returned to a church pew as if it were an old love.

I tried to rationalize my return at first, convincing myself it was curiosity – would I remember the words to the Apostle's Creed? Could the homily possibly touch me? After that, I framed it as a sort of vigil – so many city churches had already closed, I'd better visit Corpus Christi while I still could. But when I kept coming back, week after week, those excuses crumbled one at a time. I made an appointment with the spirited priest but he mistook my stammering for an ill-formed confession and I left the rectory half-absolved and more confused than ever.

Eventually I accepted that the church's pull would remain a mystery. After four and half decades of constant reinforcement my head had declared itself lonesome and begun to give way to my heart. And what my heart wanted was to go back, to look at things straight on, to take it all in – the beauty and the flaws – and see what it would be like to not leave.

So there I was at Corpus Christi. The name of the parish had changed. The congregation and priests had changed. I had changed. I sat there on Sunday mornings looking toward Our Lady of Mt. Carmel. She was crowned and sweet-faced. Her feet rested on a star-studded globe. With her darker features and more exuberant beauty, the new statue was better suited to the increasingly diverse congregation and was certainly more magnificent. Why then did my thoughts return to the statue of the Blessed Mother I'd looked to as a child – the humble Virgin whose robe was the exact shade of a morning glory?

3

Real Presence

It's like exiting an aircraft, the way the people unravel from church seats to join the Communion line. Except here, everyone waits. Even the man who trembles like a rabbit at the end of the pew would not consider stepping into the aisle until everyone in front of him has done so. Which is why we're halfway through the Communion hymn before I realize my legs won't give.

"Go ahead," I smile to the woman behind me and sit back down.

In a larger congregation my sitting might go undetected. Here, ninety people are spread among ten times as many seats and those who don't go up might as well advertise on billboards. How strange I must look and how sad, a woman sitting alone and mooning at stained glass while others head toward the altar. Only I'm not as alone as I appear. A girl in a white dress is lodged somewhere between my lungs and my gut and keeps me company in the pew. She's not totally responsible for sending me back to Mass – though ghosts have more pull than one might suppose, and it's she who's homed in on this particular church and she who would very much like to receive.

Not yet, I think. We have a history with the place, yes, but I'm here with new eyes and habit alone is no longer reason enough to partake. I'm not sure what I believe when it comes to the Eucharist and the doctrine of Real Presence, which says that God is right there in what was a second before merely a circle of bread.

Pan de Vida, the choir sings. *Bread of Life.* They alternate between English and Spanish as the microphone occasionally sputters. An off-key voice crowds out the others and splits tendrils of Spanish into rough-hewn timber as I consider the larger Church – the ongoing problems, my many misgivings, the mystifying dogma. The girl pushes in for a better view and settles smack dab in the middle of my chest, and the feel of her there – with her long hair and hopeful green barrettes – adds a spritz of melancholy to the doubts which multiply and swoop like a flock of wayward starlings over my head.

The next Sunday I push toward the center aisle to join the others, but when the exiting of pews unwinds my way, fear takes over and I sit back down. The homily and readings are inspiring enough to justify my weekly trips but, as the weeks tick by, my sitting solidifies into habit. I think back to the days when I simply stood and received and did not think so much about such things. I begin to despair and threaten myself, saying: *If you don't go up this time, don't bother coming back.* But threats never work in cases of love; Communion, it turns out, is a case of love, and the following week I slink again into my seat. She's still with me, the child I once was, smoothing the folds of her old dress while waiting for the day we'll rejoin the line, say "amen," and feel a little fuller as we head back to our seat.

Every week the others stand. Every week I add my voice to *Pan de Vida* or *Gentle Mother* while watching them process to the altar: the curmudgeonly man whose features look to have been chiseled from granite; the ladies who pass hand sanitizer between them after the Sign of Peace; the mother and daughter with beautiful hair who whisper like sisters during Mass. I study their shuffles and strides and slow steps until I've memorized the backs of nearly everyone at church.

Like this my Sundays march on. Until a morning in late February when there are fewer people overall – or the handful of others who don't go up have stayed home. Either way, my sitting throbs in the face of the church. The girl loops her hand around my wrist and lassoes me back to the weeks before my First Communion. How excited I'd been, counting down the days as though it were Christmas. I shake the memory away, place my palms flat against the pew, and, just when I think I might crumble from the weight of separation, the priest stands without warning and walks to the front of the sanctuary.

You see, he says, motioning toward the altar. *It's all so simple. Bread and wine. A table set.*

It was Angie who convinced me to have a First Communion. My family had moved away during the years I would have celebrated the sacrament, and when we reappeared in the neighborhood a few years later my mother did not immediately return to the Catholic church. But my old friend Angie was still living nearby and I followed her back to Corpus Christi, where, after I made a hangdog face while watching her stand with the others, she said: "Go see Father Jim about having a First Communion."

Some kids were bold in games of hopscotch or mother may I, but Angie was bold in everything. She knew without a doubt she'd escape the neighborhood before the rest of us even understood what that meant. "She's a snob," other kids said. Snobbery was one of the worst offenses anyone could commit in a place where most families lived without working cars and everyone ate free lunches at school. Better to be branded a liar or a cheat.

"You can borrow my dress." Angie had shown off the froth of white satin before, pointing out its ruffled neckline and the tulle overlay of its skirt. Its sheer sleeves stopped midway to my wrists and the skirt barely covered my knees, but to me it was pure extravagance, and I turned inside out with desire to wear it. The dress swayed me more than the sacrament, so I bolstered myself with a bit of Angie's backbone and went to see the priest.

It was arranged. A Thursday night folk Mass that fall. Most First Communions are group affairs on Sundays in spring, but I wore Angie's dress as the leaves on the locust trees went gold along Prince Street. Angie's veil was gone by then, or too precious to lend, so I begged my mother for money to buy a pack of barrettes from Rite-Aid in Goodman Plaza and clipped them into my hair. My knees knocked as I read from the scriptures, but my mother was back at church at least. Father Jim had insisted on her permission, which resulted in her returning to Corpus Christi armed with a cake for the party parishioners had planned. There would be punch and even presents – though as I stood there mangling the names of Hebrew tribes while reading at the altar I did not know to expect such grand things.

My family was the poorest in whatever enclave of poor families we lived. That was our one consistency. On Lamont Place only the Fayres seemed poorer, and this had less to do with their access to material goods than their constant clawing at the world. The sisters followed us to church once or twice, roving over the railroad bridge. They swaggered into the sanctuary, laughed during the homily, and gorged on cookies during the coffee hour after Mass. Naturally it was the Fayres we thought of with various levels of anger and pity as we descended into the hall and found it wiped clean of gifts.

The adults murmured and buzzed. *The Communion gifts*, they shook their heads. *Stolen*. When we'd finally settled enough to eat the cake which had been in the kitchen and was saved, parishioners expressed their sorrow while we worked our way through layers of custard and buttercream. A few described the items they'd intended for me and talked about the replacements they'd do their best to find – a white leatherette Bible, a seed pearl rosary, cards stuffed with cash.

I had not yet gotten over the thrill of wearing Angie's dress, and the idea of presents hadn't had sufficient time to root itself to my head. They were gone before I knew they were there. Things come and go. I was nine years old but practically a philosopher when it came to this. We moved more than other families, abandoning kitchens and bedrooms just as my feet fitted themselves to the warp of the floor. All of it comes and goes. Backyards and classrooms and even First Communions. I stood in the church basement in my borrowed dress, quiet and watching – and because I did not make a fuss, believed I'd let the gifts go.

Angie wasn't the only one to leave the neighborhood. Most everyone I grew up with eventually left – or tried to anyhow. Now, on a hot day in late summer, I snake through streets of collapsing porches, weedy yards, and young men on front stoops in the middle of the day. Hand-painted *For Rent* signs are tacked onto windows covered in plywood. The neighborhood looks to me the way others must have always seen it. Discarded, broken, empty. When had I become an outsider? I wonder as I'm stopped at a light on North Goodman Street and a flurry of motion catches my eye.

A young man with a stroller. Stopped and facing a child who waits as he tries to open a Freeze Pop, he does his best to tear into the plastic strip. The girl looks up, expectant, as he struggles. He puts everything he has into it – bending the plastic back and forth, shaking the entire strip – but it does not give. He tries a fingernail, then a tooth, until finally he manages to rip enough of the wrapper away to release the sweet frozen juice. A small moment, really. A hungry child; a man trying to provide. But before the light turns green and we return to our respective worlds, the moment slows down and unfolds into unexpected largeness until there's only the certainty with which the child waits, the care the man takes in lowering the treat into the stroller, and the gratitude that writes itself so fully onto their faces it's impossible to tell who has given and who has received. They blossom with joy. And for a split second the joy envelops the corner of Clifford and Goodman – the street signs and the pre-pay phone place, the liquor store and the old hardware shop, until there's no longer a man and child, or a woman sitting wide-eyed at a light. There's only the feel of everything opening and spilling into each other – the cells of our hands, the granules of tar shingles, the particles of blue sky.

These become my catechism: a man and child in northeast Rochester; a girl in a long-gone dress, a priest extending his hand toward the altar. *We're welcomed to table,* he'd recently said, *by welcoming others to it.* God is a verb, I think he was saying. Love is not a dissertation. I'm ripe, I suppose, for the final lesson, which arrives in the shape of a familiar face.

"I didn't know you were here today," Jo Lombardo says as she leans in for a hug.

"I sit in the back." I try to make my voice breezy, as if hiding in the back of a church makes sense.

"Oh," Jo says. "But I didn't see you in line for Communion."

I've known Jo since I was a child. She and her husband organized activities for neighborhood kids and made us feel at home. Sam was all bighearted gusto and Jo was selfless elegance. Theirs was undoubtedly one of the gifts stolen from my First Communion. Jo stands before me now all hazel eyes and wide smile, looking as pretty as she did back in 1978. There's no judgment in her voice. Jo is a eucharistic minister at church, carries Communion to residents in nursing homes after Mass, and probably understands better than anyone about real presence. *I didn't see you in line.* Her words echo what's been working its way through me for months. I can push through the front doors, swoon over old statues, and sing a thousand *Alleluias,* but I'm not back at church until I receive.

I think of my First Communion and the sisters who probably stole the gifts. Like crows, those girls, reducing everything to its basic substance. Poverty's cruelest trick is turning human beings into ravenous birds. And just like that she's with me again, the girl I used to be, reminding me who I am. Yes, church had captivated me as a child, but hadn't I also been drawn by hunger? I thought I'd let those stolen gifts go better than any-one, but all these years later here I am still tracing the shape of their absence. Didn't I also have my eye so fixed on crumbs I'd nearly missed out on the feast? I'd left the neighborhood and tried my best to cultivate a life far from the constraints of a grumbling stomach – except here I was, stalking the grain of ancient tables while carting around a hungry ghost.

The next time I'm at church it's Palm Sunday. Lilies bloom at the altar, palm fronds are set like strips of spring into our hands. The priest sings the consecration. His prayer sails up to the rafters and reverberates throughout the sanctuary. His voice cracks near the end, splinters from overuse. Something about this – the lone human voice breaking while lifted in song – results in a strand of sound so tender I can only close my eyes.

I open my eyes and look around. It's a familiar place – one I know better than any other. It's changed on the surface, yes. The congregation has been divided, died, or moved on, as have the priests and monsignors and bishops. The church has even been given another name. But what can that change of its essence? Who can say it's no longer Corpus Christi? Nothing of consequence can ever be taken, I realize, nor forcibly retrieved. People can sneak into church basements, push gifts into a bag, gather greeting cards and break their gummy seals while choking on laughter and the chug of their own breath. They can slip seed-pearl rosaries into their pockets, exchange dollars for candy and cigarettes and bottles of cheap wine, but still and all, Communion has not been touched.

When the Communion hymn starts up, we stand and approach the altar one at a time: the cantankerous stone-faced man, the ladies with newly sanitized hands, the mother and daughter with lustrous russet waves, and the one who sits near the back holding conversations with ghosts, who has, after all these months, finally decided to join them.

The priest's back stoops from years of bending toward others. I fix my eye on the bread he offers but see something else besides – something I had not noticed before. The girl senses it too and settles along the perimeters of my heart as he leans in, luminous. And, for a moment, we all flare – break right open and shimmer – as he sets the Body into open hands.

4

Feast of Corpus Christi

The bridge is festooned with girls in white dresses.

An assemblage of ruffles and garlands and veils, the girls scatter rose petals as they round the corner near Galway Cathedral and turn toward Nuns' Island. Similar lines of girls march throughout Ireland, leaving a trail of blossoms in their wake as they file past cemeteries and stone houses, past uncles on pub stools and pharmacies lit with green crosses, down walkways and mossy paths into inlets and beaches and bays – a cavalcade of tiny brides against the backdrop of the sea.

Back on the bridge a voice from the loudspeaker starts an Our Father, and we tourists jump at the jolt of unexpected sound. The procession carries on. An old man shuffles past, bearing a rosary in one hand and a cane in the other. Bent forty-five degrees, he sees primarily blacktop and roses as they land. A grandmother pushes a stroller. A woman in an African head wrap marches with a straight back, images of Our Lady of Guadalupe repeated on the pattern of her cobalt dress. A man staggers along, red-faced and hair-mussed, looking as if he's been jostled from a bench in nearby Kennedy Park. They come and they come, beads in their fingers, prayer on their tongues. Holding up the rear: a black-uniformed priest in a Roman hat; a Franciscan in a brown robe; a trio of diocesan clerics in white chasubles. Behind them, the heart of the procession. A swinging censer incenses the air, followed by four marchers, each carrying a corner pole of a tasseled canopy over the celebrant. Outfitted in layers of ecclesiastical gold, the priest holds the monstrance aloft. It's like the sun come down to earth, the gilded vessel in Father's hands, and he conveys it with the vigilance of a mother carrying a newborn in her arms. At the center of the sunburst is a circle of glass the size of a Host – the luna, it's called – the nucleus of the monstrance in which the Blessed Sacrament is held and exposed.

By the time the procession takes its final turn toward the Poor Clare Monastery, the girls in white dresses have spent their roses, and the canopy bearers no longer keep time – the square of fringed silk sags as they wind past a small table set with flowers and a waist-high statue of the Sacred Heart of Jesus. They march on, reciting Hail Marys as they follow the bend of the Lower Corrib River where salmon make their way upstream as they've done since the time salmon began.

If he'd been in Galway that day, Martin Luther would have seen the banners coming over the bridge and turned with quick footsteps in the direction of the docks. If he was especially crotchety – from lack of sleep or the unexpected bite of Irish sun – he might twist his face, shout *Blasphemy!*, and try to persuade those with rosaries of the error of their ways.

Celebrated sixty days after Easter, the Feast of Corpus Christi observes the mysterious change at Mass from bread and wine to Body and Blood. Since the thirteenth century the day has been marked by communal processions and eucharistic benedictions – and more than the doctrine of transubstantiation, it was the public aspect of the feast that provoked Luther's ire: *At no festival are God and his Christ more blasphemed than on this day, and particularly by the procession. For then people are treating the Blessed Sacrament with such ignominy that it becomes only play-acting and is just vain idolatry.*

Anglicans were less inflammatory but just as committed in their objection: *The Sacraments were not ordained of Christ to be gazed upon, or to be carried about, but that we should duly use them.*

The reformers rightly sounded the alarm against an elaborate but empty spirituality, but veered so far in the other direction that they demonized devotion itself. What they called play-acting, Catholics saw as reverence. What they considered idolatry, Catholics regarded as affection. The Roman Church, with its dogged insistence on the physical manifestation of the divine, fostered a tradition that, for better and worse, remained bound to the body – its pains and joys, its goodness and confusions and longings.

So it was with Corpus Christi. The Eucharist was not merely a symbol made sacred by its time on the altar, but God Himself, the Body of Christ. And where God is present, devotion must follow. The tradition of walking with the Blessed Sacrament through the center of town thrived for centuries in Catholic countries, including the United States. Only in the past century has the custom begun to evaporate and, in many places, all but died. The cantankerous Luther would be delighted to learn that fewer girls scatter rose petals along main streets every year.

Because it was the name of my childhood church, I knew Corpus Christi meant the *Body of Christ* but saw it primarily as punishment of syllables on the mouth.

Corpus Crispy, we said in the neighborhood, making our church sound more like breakfast cereal than the body we saw portrayed in the stations every week at church. As in Galway we had a bridge near our church – but instead of a river, it passed over the Goodman Street railroad yards, with nothing but old trains and wayward pedestrians streaming beneath it. Despite our parish name we did not celebrate the Feast of Corpus Christi by walking through the neighborhood with priest and canopy and monstrance. By the time I received the Eucharist in the late 1970s such fixings were considered old-fashioned. The only place we processed was down the church's center aisle – first, held by our parents at baptism; then again at First Communion;

later at confirmations and wedding days; and, later still, laid out in coffins and carried again by those who loved us best.

I became an altar girl soon after my First Communion. I slipped into the clean white robe and knotted the cincture around my waist. I used the long-armed brass snuffer to extinguish tapers after Mass and rang the altar bells as the priest elevated the Host and again as he lifted the chalice. Sometimes too I bore the cross at the start of service, leading lectors and priest down the center aisle. But though I went to church twice a week – sometimes more – I did not concern myself with philosophical conundrums and theological constructs. If *Corpus Christi* was a fistfight in a child's mouth, *transubstantiation* was an all-out brawl. When it came to the Body of Christ, the summer my sister stole a Communion wafer provided my most extended rumination.

The large stone building was cool after the steamy walk down North Goodman to East Main and over the railroad bridge. We were early, with no one else in sight. Steph strode to the offertory table where the plate and carafe were covered, lifted the cloth, and popped a wafer into her mouth. My sister was braver, in general, and when it came to matters of religion more firmly unconvinced. I stood there, marveling at her pluck while glancing around the empty church in case we might be caught. I looked toward the high altar and back to my dark-haired sister as she swallowed a wafer so thin it was practically air. God was not in the wafer, according to the rules, but I was not sure where He might be. What did it mean for God to be part of the knowable touchable world – and if He was so alive in the tabernacle that we must genuflect when we passed, wasn't He alive outside it as well? In the lilac blooming in our backyard, for instance, or in the family fighting next door – even in my sister's hand as she reached under the cloth and came away with a translucent circle of bread?

Despite my indifference when it came to Corpus Christi, my time on the altar was not wasted. The rhythm and splendor of the Mass seeped in through my eyes and ears and even my nose until they imprinted onto each of my cells. The weight of the globed cruets in my palms; the gleam of the polished chalice; the motion of the paten going back and forth in my hands as I stood beside the priest, extending the brass plate under the chins of those who still received by mouth in case any particle should fall.

How clearly I can see the parishioners coming to Communion: the bend of their heads as they arrive one at a time; the certainty of their *Amens* and the flutter of hands as they cross themselves and turn away; the sound of their heels clicking on tile as they return to their seats; the creak of wood as they lower themselves onto kneelers and let their foreheads come to rest in open hands.

When else did we bow to something larger than ourselves? Where else had I seen faces so open and solemn that tears sometimes came into their eyes? On television, perhaps, when actors played the part of being in love. In movies. Or books. But in our neighborhood, where most fathers were absent and mothers worried over the steady onslaught of bills and raged some days and laughed the next – even on those days when we managed to be peaceful or glad – no face ever looked as tender as it did in the Communion line.

Back in Galway city, the procession arrives at the monastery doors. The girls in white dresses slay with their softness. Like kittens. Like bunnies. Like fawns. The old men remove their hats as the priest begins the benediction. A toddler with a face like fresh cream flits in and out of her grandmother's lap, but most bend their heads, or go to their knees, as the priest gives the blessing. *Tantum Ergo*, they sing. *O Sacrament Most Holy*.

Afterwards, people wander around the grounds. The Poor Clares are cloistered and the monastery is open only for the Feast of Corpus Christi. A rare event, to get inside. People peek into the chapel and photograph each other under flowering trees.

An old man in a blazer too hot for June traipses around the little greenhouse looking through the glass at tomato plants and herbs, marveling, perhaps, at how such lushness can flourish behind closed doors.

Maybe he's thinking of the Poor Clares, of his own garden, or fretting over the fate of tradition, on this day when old people in Galway's procession outnumber young people three to one. Or else he's looking so deeply into a flowering thyme that he sees himself as a boy walking behind his cousins who wear dresses his own mother helped to sew. It's possible he's looking into the greenhouse but seeing his childhood home along the coast; the whole of the town stepping from St. Patrick's, the strangeness of thurible and candles out in the open, the grand canopy and priests in their finery strolling down the main street toward the bay. He's remembering, perhaps, the sound of prayer against a backdrop of foxglove and dog roses; the flaxen cows spread like enormous goddesses near stone walls. He's recalling the empty lot beside Doyle's shop where the fuchsia grows and Mrs. Horan watching from the front of her cottage, tufts of dark hair lifted by the breeze, the baby in her arms caught in afternoon light and the sea itself blue as the Blessed Mother's cape. He's remembering the people and places he passed every day and how different they looked on the Feast of Corpus Christi – were they made beautiful by the priest and the canopy or did walking with the Blessed Sacrament only cause him to better notice what was always there? How true everything looked and how full. The whole of the town turned out to carry God among the common things – the lot of them lighting the trees and shops and rooftops with the lantern of their attention until everywhere they stepped became church.

SEARCH FOR THE VIRGIN, PART III

Rochester

The search is casual at first.

When I spy the gentle slope of a head through a window while walking to my car one Sunday after Mass, I turn back and sneak into the sacristy, heart thumping, but it's not her. I survey the basement the following week, sniff around locked confessionals, and slip into the vestry where I find a foot-high Mary in a sky-blue robe and a Virgin of Guadalupe lying on her side – but my Lady is not there.

Except for the rectory, which is kept locked and unoccupied, I've checked the entire church. Anyone with sense would stop there.

Instead I redouble my efforts and make myself into a combination of Church Lady and Nancy Drew. What is this attachment? I wonder even as I pursue her. Is she the parent I'd always longed for – one who cannot speak harsh words, move away, or otherwise disappoint? Is she a symbol of the community that was once closer than family? An emblem of childhood and all things lost?

Like my return to church itself, my devotion is impossible to figure. Even in my years of lapsing I'd remained connected to Mary. I'd see her in museums and chapels and garden grottoes and feel the air flicker between us. It was not so much adoration as an instinctive response to an image of comfort and beauty that had surrounded me during the most formative years of my life. But the connection has grown or else my awareness of it has increased – it's possible I loved her all along and it took the shock of her absence to remind me how much.

"You should check with the diocese," the sacristan advises when I ask where the statue might have ended up. She tells me the name of the person who handles the merging of churches and transfer of sacred objects. After a few tries, the woman responds to my email with a photograph of a life-sized Mary rising from the basement of Corpus Christi on a wheelchair lift. An Our Lady of Grace model with a cape the color of sky.

The Corpus Christi Mary! The Virgin of Prince Street. My Lady, true and blue.

The statue had been sold to a church in the neighboring diocese of Buffalo, she writes, but isn't sure which one. When I ask if there are records and whether I can check them, she says she'll have to get back to me. But either she's busy or has tired of my statue talk because I don't hear from her again. In the meantime my wheels are spinning. Why would a Buffalo parish need a statue of the Blessed Mother? That the neighboring diocese has had even more church closings than Rochester should mean a surplus of Buffalo Virgins.

After sending a reminder email and hearing nothing back, I begin to wonder if there's something I've overlooked – a reluctance to discuss the sale of sacred objects, perhaps, the emotional work of merging churches, some lingering sensitivity about Corpus Christi's history, or ongoing touchiness related to the parish in local Catholic circles. Objects become touchstones for particular places, after all, and the statue represents not only the Blessed Mother but the trajectory and disposition of the church in which she stood for seventy-five years.

Only now am I struck by how lucky I was to find Corpus Christi open at all.

Parish closures have become common throughout the Northeast as shifting demographics have led to dwindling congregations, fewer priests, and buildings too numerous to maintain. As local factories downsized or died and the descendants of the immigrants who'd come to work in them moved away, dioceses in the former industrial hubs of upstate New York were hit especially hard. The northeast section of Rochester was once home to seventeen Catholic parishes – each with its own architecture, history, and traditions. Germans were followed by Irish, then Sicilians and Poles, and, later, Eastern Europeans, African Americans, and Puerto Ricans. One at a time neighborhood churches were built and consecrated and filled. One at a time their doors closed until only a few remained. One of these is Corpus Christi.

In many ways Corpus Christi is typical. Formed in 1888, the parish began in a modest brick building used jointly as a school. The population exploded as new arrivals came west on the Erie Canal and settled the areas east of the Genesee River. By 1903 the parish had expanded into the larger and newly built sandstone church on the corners of East Main and Prince Streets. Attendance peaked in the forties and fifties, but the flush of prosperity was followed by postwar suburban flight, and by the 1960s the parish had begun its battle to survive. And like other neighborhood churches, Corpus Christi's statue of the Blessed Virgin graced its sanctuary throughout it all.

Mary looked on as babies were baptized, couples married, and coffins incensed and lifted from the church. Her features did not change as broad Irish accents gave way to the honeyed cluck of Sicilian and tender rivulets of Spanish. Candles flickered at her feet through the Great Depression and World War II, as telephone lines were installed along Prince and buses replaced trolleys on East Main. She offered refuge as race riots erupted in nearby streets and kept watch during the long years of Vietnam. She was there as parishioners celebrated their annual bonuses and, years later, when they came to grieve the pink slips the factories doled out in their place. She'd outlasted priests and presidents and popes; weathered ice storms, heat waves, and power outages; even persevered through the nationally publicized schism that eventually tore the parish apart.

After all those years she's gone. Unaccounted for. Lost somewhere in Buffalo.

Instead of taking the lack of specific information from the diocese as a sign to let the matter drop, the mystery emboldens me. I want to know where she ended up. I want to see her one more time. I want to know that her robe is as blue as I remember and her hands are still open after all this time. If Corpus Christi's early history is emblematic of other parishes, then the whereabouts of its Virgin Mary means something too.

I know I'm unlikely to succeed, and see by their expressions that my desire to launch a full-scale statue search makes no sense to anyone else. But some of the most important things in life make no sense, and whether I'm able to find Mary or not is hardly the point. The point is that I need to try.

5

Altar Girl

Jacinia breezes along the aisles, gathering kisses from the ladies seated in pews.

Bendición, they say as she bends into them. *God bless you*, she says in return. The possibility that someone might not welcome her does not enter her head. She tries to remember what she's been told and stops herself from running in church. Instead, she skips into the vestry and returns in a flash, brown skin luminous against a white robe. On the altar are polished chalices and cut-glass cruets and a cluster of brass *sanctus* bells. Jacinia outshines them all.

She spies the parish priest and races his way. She's a small girl and he's as tall as a tree. *Padre Bob!* she says and wraps herself around the trunk of his leg. That he's talking to someone else, that he's not as quickly or easily demonstrative in his affection – these are not her concerns. She finds the other server and moves with him to the back of the church. They stand there, a quiet boy and an electric girl, waiting for the priest in his flowing vestments and the two deacons – one with the silver Jesus hair, and the other who elevates the gilded *Book of the Gospels* over his tremendous belly – to begin the procession down the aisle.

In some places she could not exist. While the American church, by and large, has come to accept female servers, they are not universally embraced. The Vatican allowed wiggle room on the matter in 1983 and officially dropped its ban in 1994 when it allowed but did not require that female servers be invited to assist during Mass. The decision was left to bishops, who, in turn, often left it to pastors. Only one United States diocese (Lincoln, Nebraska) prohibits girls entirely, though individual parishes and pastors have elected not to use them.

A few years ago the pastor of Star of the Sea Church in San Francisco announced his plan to eliminate female servers. "Boys usually end up losing interest because girls generally do a better job," the priest said, and more importantly: "Altar service is intrinsically tied to the priesthood and serves as feeder programs for the seminary."

His view echoes one of the most conservative voices in the Church. Cardinal Raymond Burke has also charged that allowing girls on the altar has hurt vocations.

"Young boys don't want to do things with girls. It's just natural," Burke said at about the same time. The focus on women's issues has led the church to become "very feminized," according to Burke, who claimed this turned off men who "respond to rigor and precision and excellence."

In the early 1980s the Bishop of Rochester took the radical position that women were equal to men. In his first pastoral letter Bishop Matthew Clark issued a ninety-two-point treatise highlighting the historic and problematic uneasiness of clergy relative to women, while championing their increased role: *They wish to be acknowledged as full members of the Church*, Clark wrote, *but they wish this joy also for every member of the Church, male or female, lay person, priest, deacon or religious.*

Local churches were encouraged to assign women more visible roles, which included increasing their presence on the altar. Because canon law dictates that only the ordained can deliver homilies and because Rome forbids their ordination, women are precluded from preaching by design. Bishop Clark understood this but invited parishes to be creative, which allowed women to offer post-Gospel reflections in consultation with pastors and amounted to *de facto* preaching.

But even before Clark became bishop, a dynamic young priest assigned to my parish welcomed women into leadership roles. Twenty-nine-year-old Father Jim Callan was a gifted speaker, and so were the women he invited to preach. So gifted, I've spent years trying to find homilies of the same caliber. I've had to look hard because in the past two decades a shift occurred in the church hierarchy as Clark and similarly inclined bishops were replaced. Women's voices were silenced, their bodies banished again to the shadows. But back in the late 1970s and 1980s – perhaps because ours was a city church on the brink of dying and no one bothered to look closely – an air of openness flourished. Father McCabe before him had allowed girls to serve at Corpus Christi when no boys were available, as pinch hitters of sorts, but Father Callan became the first in the city, and in the region perhaps, to regularly welcome girls to serve at Mass.

That is how I came to be an altar girl.

My favorite thing was to ring the handheld bells and cause sound to soar to the rafters and throughout the church as first the Body was elevated, then the Blood. This is a moment so wondrous, the bells said, words will not do. After that, I most liked to stand beside Father Callan and push the little brass plate back and forth under the chins of parishioners as they came forward to receive Communion. The paten had a shine to it, as did the faces, and there was the chance, however slight, that the Host might drop and I'd be called upon to save the day with the nimble work of my hands.

Why then did I say to my school principal that women shouldn't be priests?

It was middle school. That might explain it. I was in Sister Eileen's office serving time for some minor infraction or had stopped by to describe the latest romantic upheaval on *General*

Hospital when somehow the topic shifted to church and she said some people believed women should be allowed to be priests.

"No way." My words reverberated throughout the office lined with shelves of old textbooks and bent file cabinets. Neat spaces, but small and worn, the offices in which legions of Catholic women labor.

"Why not?" Sister Eileen went on with what she'd been doing, straightening files or copying figures as we talked. Who knows what nonsense I muttered in reply? There was only the sense that I'd disappointed her – not in my opinion so much as in my lack of thought. I enjoyed the rare privilege of serving on a Catholic altar and listening to women preach but never once considered that a woman might preside at Mass.

No way, I'd said. A girl from a single-parent home, the daughter of a mother who refused makeup, went bow-hunting, and regularly rejected social conventions. Was my need for father figures so profound I could not risk muddling the one place where they were routinely offered? Was I so used to men in the most important roles – presidents and mayors and popes – that by age twelve I'd already lost the ability to imagine a woman leading a country, a city, a church?

Grown-ups, it turned out, could be every bit as reactive as a middle school girl.

Rochester's bishop continued to welcome women into leadership roles. As vocations to the priesthood diminished, women took on formerly priestly functions such as pastoral counseling, liturgical planning, and carrying the Eucharist to nursing homes and hospitals. This was the case in many churches, but at Corpus Christi women became increasingly active on the altar. People began to grumble. The loudest complaints came from outside the parish, a small but vocal contingent who longed for a return to "tradition" – by which they did not mean the original tradition of Christianity as an inclusive band of radicals who threatened the establishment, but the status quo hundreds of years later, when the Church had solidified into the establishment itself and the closest the female body got to the altar was to set out flowers and dust candlesticks.

That Father Callan and his lead associate, Mary Ramerman, were not timid only magnified matters as Mary inched her way into spaces reserved for men. First she read the gospel and delivered homilies. Next she began to wear priestly vestments, to lift the chalice at the consecration, to hear confessions. If that weren't enough, there was an air about her. Entitlement, some might say. A well-developed backbone and unwillingness to take a back seat. The makings of a fine pastor, perhaps, but in a woman such qualities are harder to take – though a woman without such qualities would squander her time waiting to be permitted into sacred space. Over the centuries how many gifted women had done just that?

The bishop came under fire by both camps. At one extreme his liberalism was blamed for the disintegration of local Catholicism, while at the other there was outrage he didn't further his progressive stance. Things reached a fever pitch. Outsiders sneaked into Corpus Christi with cameras and tape recorders to gather evidence of infractions, which they included in letters of complaint to Cardinal Ratzinger's Congregation for the Doctrine of the Faith in Rome.

In the end Bishop Clark was charged with bringing the parish back in line. His reassignment of Father Callan caused a firestorm. Most of the thousands who'd joined the parish during his tenure rebelled. Whether the various attempts at reconciliation were thwarted or half-hearted to begin with, they eventually failed, and in 1999 Father Callan and his former staff formed a new church (Spiritus Christi), causing a schism that made national headlines.

For Catholics it was a battle without victors. Those who'd pushed for what they saw as orthodoxy were appeased, perhaps, that after twenty-two years Father Callan was ousted and Mary Ramerman gone along with him. They would no longer have to trouble themselves with the image of a woman daring to stand at the center of a Catholic church. In their new parish Father Callan and Mary Ramerman continued their work – attracting new parishioners and expanding outreach programs, finding that those they sheltered and fed did not concern themselves with the parish's standing with Rome. Meanwhile the diocese lost its most dynamic flock, thousands of committed and generous parishioners who'd staffed and funded vigorous social justice programs, including a homeless shelter and hospice, community health clinics, and prison programs. In one week alone parish collections plummeted from $24,000 to $7,000. Within months more pews were vacant than when the dynamic young priest had arrived two decades before. These days male clerics have the pulpit all to themselves, but increasingly preach to rows of empty seats.

Cardinal Burke presided at Mass when I was in Ireland two summers ago.

He was attended by boys in lace frocks and men in heavily brocaded chasubles who displayed varying levels of deference depending on level and rank. They genuflected and knelt, incensed the spaces around him, and carried his crozier as he walked. They bowed deeply and removed the Cardinal's miter as he sat in his throne, then bowed deeply again and put it back on. On and off went the hat, here and there swung the censer, as the group of men buzzed about the altar.

I was teaching in Cork that summer and had come to SS. Peter and Paul's to hear an Irish Mass. The usher noticed me, a stranger in the last row, and came over: "Now if you'll stick around, you'll see something special, a High Mass celebrated by Cardinal Burke himself."

I'd already sat through one Mass and decided to stay for the next. The stew of Celtic syllables had been undecipherable, but the Irish Mass had engaged me at least. Now the men on the altar behaved as if on an island. The disconnection was mutual.

People came in to light candles and let the doors thud behind them as they rattled about with strollers and crinkling parcels. Worshippers arrived throughout the service and traipsed down the center aisle in swishy jackets and high-heeled shoes.

I thought of the jewelry box I once had, whose plastic ballerina popped up the moment the lid was opened and stopped dancing the moment it closed. The jewelry box didn't last long. It wasn't well made and I never had anything suitable to put inside it. But back when it was still around, I'd occasionally get caught up by the spinning fluff of the ballerina's skirt. So pretty, I'd think, but watching her was always a lonely prospect as she was drawn to nothing so much as the sight of her own turning in the mirror and never once looked back.

One cannot be shocked when cardinals like Burke or Ratzinger oppose women on the altar. But to the disappointment of many, even the much beloved Pope Francis has ruled out female priests. In response to shrinking vocations, the Pope has indicated an openness to reevaluating mandatory clerical celibacy rather than considering female ordination, suggesting that even the most progressive of recent pontiffs can better envision the loss of the much-touted tradition of celibacy (with its own admonishments of the female body) to a woman presiding at the altar. It's possible he's moving slowly and must keep his intentions hidden, but he sent no hints of openness when questioned about the matter by a Swedish journalist a few years back. Instead, he invoked Pope John Paul II's 1994 letter confirming that women could never be priests:

> Wherefore, in order that all doubt may be removed regarding a matter of great importance, a matter which pertains to the Church's divine constitution itself . . . I declare that the Church has no authority whatsoever to confer priestly ordination on women and that this judgment is to be definitively held by all the Church's faithful.

Pope Francis, referring to the letter, said: "John Paul II had the last clear word on this, and it stands."

Most who oppose the female body on the altar don't claim that women aren't worthy. Women are simply different, they say, and throw their hands in the air while declaring allegiance to divine law. Jesus never chose a female apostle, they charge, while allowing themselves to forget – at least for the moment – Jesus's radical message of inclusion, the fact that he consistently chose it over the established rules and counted women among his most trusted friends.

In the same interview with the Swedish writer, Pope Francis, perhaps feeling dogged by the female problem, invoked Mary: "People ask me: 'Who is more important in the theology or in the spirituality of the church, the apostles or Mary, on the day of Pentecost?'"

"It is Mary," the good pope said, and must have felt his answer was a gift.

Mary's popularity reaches beyond the Church. Even ex-Catholics often respond favorably to her image. When I attended the Feast of Guadalupe Mass at Corpus Christi this past December, the visiting priest told the story of Our Lady's apparitions outside Mexico City in 1531. She'd appeared not to a king or even a cleric but to the peasant Juan Diego. With dark skin and black hair, the Virgin spoke not the Spanish of European conquerors but the native Nahuatl. The priest continued on, singing Our Lady's praises. *Nuestra Señora*, he preached in Spanish, *the most important of women. Without sin. A model of piety, faith, and grace.*

But, he admonished, *María no es Dios*. Mary is not God.

He said it several times, slow and loud, enunciating every syllable. I'd heard the message before, of course: Mary was a vessel, the bringer of God, and not God herself. But the way the young priest said it – the very weight of his correction – made it seem as if the mere suggestion that Mary might be divine was somehow insulting to God.

Everyone sat for the duration of Mass and, apart from Communion and the Sign of Peace, remained politely contained in their seats. The church did not come alive, really, until the end, when children in peasant shirts and embroidered dresses formed a line and, one at a time, approached the altar and left bundles of roses before an oversized image of Our Lady of Guadalupe. Adults came forward too, wearing T-shirts and ponchos emblazoned with her image. On the way into church I'd passed a truck with decals of *la Virgen* on its bumper, side panels, and rear glass. I thought of trips to Mexico where *la Virgen* reigns supreme. Surrounded by sunbursts and crowned with stars, she dangles from necklaces and rear-view mirrors. Her image is painted onto cowboy boots and teacups, bedazzled onto denim jackets, and carved onto the center of dining room tables. She's tattooed onto forearms, ankles, and the delicate patch of skin inside the wrist. As I was dining with a friend in a restaurant in San Miguel de Allende, our waiter revealed a peek of Our Lady's mantle near his collarbone – the radiant tip of an image of *la Virgen* which he smiled and explained bloomed over the entire plain of his chest.

"I used to be an altar girl," I say to Jacinia. "A long time ago, in this church."

I'm sitting in back where she and the quiet boy wait for the priest and the deacons to line up.

"You were?" She raises her brows.

I nod, but don't tell her I wasn't a good one, that the priest suggested at several junctures that I reconsider my calling – but only because I was never quite comfortable with so many eyes on me. Perhaps that's why I liked the bells so much, and the ability to make a joyous noise while hidden behind the altar cloth.

I don't say this to Jacinia. Nor do I say that it was breaking the rules for a girl to stand so near the tabernacle in those days.

I don't say that our priest had been brave, that it had meant something to be admitted into such sacred space, that I might be worthy of it somehow.

Things change in a heartbeat. Not the Church perhaps — though given the empty pews and the ongoing anger over clerical transgressions, it will continue to harden and crumble or must eventually give way. Who knows what Catholicism will look like by the time Jacinia wanders into her late forties and begins to question what it all means? I see her then, the future Jacinia, pushing through the Main Street doors and making her way down the center aisle, remembering the ladies with their kisses and the blue candles flickering in a rack near the statue of Our Lady, the way it seemed the entire sanctuary bent to receive her.

Ah, but now the priest has arrived and the choir starts up with their tambourines and maracas. The congregation stands and claps to the strum of instruments and lively bounce of voices as the white-robed group processes down the aisle. The deacon with the long silver hair smiles as the other hoists the ornate book over the globe of his belly. Together they reach the sanctuary and bow. The boy returns the processional cross to its rack and slips with Jacinia into the seat behind the priest. He's an extraordinary priest, backbreakingly generous and alive in ways that most of us are not, but Jacinia is where the eye goes. Not because she seeks attention — she is, in fact, comfortable enough to sit back. Nor because she's pretty, for that's to be expected with little girls. No, Jacinia draws the eye because that which we come to church to pray for — she is filled with that.

6

Miracle of the Eyes

In 1985 statues across Ireland began to move.

On Valentine's Day, in the village of Asdee, seven-year-old Elizabeth Flynn was saying Hail Marys when a statue of the Sacred Heart of Jesus beckoned her with a finger. The Blessed Mother followed suit. When Elizabeth called to her sisters to tell them what she'd seen, other children flooded into the church. *Yes*, they said, *we see it too.*

A few weeks later two girls in Ballydesmond reported a statue moving in St. Patrick's Church. A village woman fainted after witnessing the same but refused to talk about it, saying: *If there's a message, it will come again and more than me will see it.*

In the seaside town of Courtmacsharry a group of tourists saw a statue move. Another was seen to breathe in a grotto on the Waterford-to-Kilkenny road. In Waterford two boys reported a statue shifting her eyes outside the Mercy Convent School, while back in Asdee an eighty-year-old farmer saw the statue of the Virgin blink three times. In Cork city three children said a statue rocked so hard they feared she'd topple. In Rathdangan Mrs. Haddie Doyle observed Our Lady smile. In Kilfinane Geraldine O'Grady noticed the throat of the Blessed Mother's statue move while Oliver Herbert reported her veil falling away to reveal a girl with long brown hair. A statue was seen to sway in Mountcollins. In Mooncoin Bernadette O'Hanlon stated that a statue of the Virgin opened its left eye while a single tear fell from the right.

In July Cathy O'Mahony stopped by the grotto at Ballinspittle to say the rosary with her two daughters when they noticed movement up the hill. Both said the Virgin's chest rose and fell as if filled with air. The next night a hundred people flocked to Ballinspittle. Some saw the Virgin change expression. Others reported seeing her wave or smile or even blush.

I looked up and saw Our Lady ascending into heaven, said Josephine Foran. *Her face became human like a baby's. It was lovely pink flesh.*

There's no shortage of statues in Ireland. Jesus is well represented, as are Saints Patrick and Brigid, but the Blessed Virgin Mary reigns supreme. When Pope Pius XII declared 1954 a Marian year, Catholics celebrated worldwide with dedications, processions, and statue coronations – but no country seems to have embraced the Queen of Heaven with such fervor as Ireland. Hundreds of grottoes sprang up along roadsides, ranging from statuettes set into simple stone niches to hillsides planted with flowers and topped with life-size statues.

The Ballinspittle Virgin was fashioned of concrete and plaster and crowned by a halo of electric light. Modeled after the apparition in Lourdes, France, she was accompanied by a statue of a kneeling Saint Bernadette, the beneficiary of Mary's visitation. Like many Marian statues in Ireland, Our Lady was installed unpainted – the demand was so great in 1954 that there was no time to add blue to their sashes before sending them out from the Cork workshop.

In a season of moving statues, Ballinspittle became the pulse point. The media descended. Thousands flocked to the grotto, outfitted with binoculars and rosaries. Even the most hardened skeptics reported movement of some sort. Some saw her hands move; at least one person reported *little birds flying in and out of Mary's crown*. Stories of cures began to circulate. Lumps disappeared from a sick child's hands. Wayward husbands returned. Bent legs straightened, and walking sticks were abandoned to the cow fields of Ballinspittle.

While the pope's declaration of the Marian year had spurred the construction of midcentury grottoes, thirty years later the church hierarchy was among the least inclined to accept the miracles. Bishop Murphy of Cork and Ross said: *Direct supernatural intervention is a very rare happening in life.* Bishop Cassidy of Clonfert worried that *with all this movement, we turn Mary into a marionette. Mary's function,* he warned, *is not to move herself, but to move us.*

But while the statues were religious in form, their movement was not bound by the authority of clerics. At Ballinspittle the crowds swelled and continued into autumn and were sizable even on Halloween night when three men pulled up, jumped from their car, and attacked the statue. They destroyed the Virgin's face with hammers and axes while taunting the pilgrims, including several nuns praying that night. The attackers were evangelical Protestants; one later said: *The statue at Ballinspittle only moved once – when I hit it. If it moves again, I'll be back.*

If the statues of Ireland were given to movement, their timing was painfully off. While they practically waltzed off their pedestals in 1985, they had been stone silent the year before, when on the last day of January, in Granard, a fifteen-year-old schoolgirl made her way toward the church. It's unclear how much anyone knew about Ann Lovett's condition as she set off for the grotto in her school uniform and gave birth surrounded by wet rock and frozen moss – a kneeling statue of Bernadette looking on as she pushed. When schoolchildren found her hours later beside her dead infant, she'd lost blood and was shivering hard.

Why did she go there, that girl? Was the statue, slick with January drizzle, the warmest place she knew? Cold to the touch, yes. Fashioned of concrete and plaster, but like cotton compared to the rest of Granard and the country that made birth control impossible and had voted to keep the ban on abortion iron-clad just a few months before. When the girl and her newborn were buried in the churchyard a few days later, people began to gossip about the coldness of priests, the silence of nuns, and the tight-lipped chill of the village as a whole. But, in the end, there was only this: the statue of the Virgin, locked in position as Ann Lovett trudged through winter fields, pain mounting with every step. *Perhaps*, she thought as she approached the church – letting herself believe in the beautiful way only the most desperate do – *perhaps Our Lady will help*.

I wonder if a statue is as real to those who don't see her move as to those who do. To the clerics who prayed before a plaster figure while closing their eyes to the flesh-and-blood bodies of girls around them. To the Protestants with hammers and picks. To the girl in the churchyard as her body began to break and flood. A statue is a repository of desire, perfect in its human likeness, but better still, because its silence does not disrupt the dogged arrow of our projections.

Just ask Pygmalion and his ivory-chiseled bride. Just ask the mob roving through Antwerp in August 1566, in what will come to be known as the *Beeldenstorm* (statue storm), men going from church to church with axes, mocking the statues of the Holy Family before pissing on them and bashing in their faces. Just ask clever Daedalus, whose wax-cemented wings famously failed when his son skimmed too close to the sun, but whose statues were said to be so perfectly sculpted they required tethering to keep them from fleeing at night.

My mother was a sucker for miracles. She liked most of all the shrine near Niagara Falls where a thirteen-foot statue of the Virgin reigned from atop a Plexiglas globe. Like the city of Niagara Falls itself, the shrine had seen better days. Gift shop shelves teemed with glow-in-the-dark rosaries and faded prayer cards, while mass-produced statuettes collected dust in the folds of shoddily painted robes. But with its candlelit chapels, beds of roses, and Avenue of the Saints – the shrine was a world away, the only vacation from the realities of her life my mother would ever get, and nearly as good as the miracles she whipped up. Like the time she cured the warts on my sister's hand through the work of her rosary group.

I think it was the Compound W, I said back then.

Maybe, she answered. *But how can you know for sure?*

Her face was wide, eyes lit like Christmas – and, like a Protestant on the streets of Belgium in the summer of 1566, I thought how easy it would be to topple her. Only now is it clear to me: the cramped dead-end street; the horde of children; the unrelenting stream of low-paying jobs. Where else could one find miracles in our neighborhood? The truth was that I would have liked to believe too, and while I didn't – at least not the way she did – I was drawn to those who did and wanted to be convinced, to allow myself a bit of wonder and the occasional pair of wax wings.

Here I must confess my own tendency toward half sight. I'm nearsighted and do not always wear my glasses. For the past few years I've ditched them altogether except for driving. This has led to many fine things: a pair of white plastic buoys floating in the Wallkill River in New Paltz became swans; a flower the exact shade of a bluebird's wing blossomed from a water valve on a late summer walk; a prickly pear grove in Sicily became an orchard studded with pomegranates.

Even when we wear our prescribed lenses, our vision is always playing tricks. Longing conspires with refracted light. Desire fattens the eye. We're granted the merciful blur of cursory sight – and how lovely the blur. How kindly the question mark, all curve and bend and semicircle crown, especially compared to the period with its tightfisted declarations. Of course, the true shape of the thing must eventually emerge. The buoys in the Wallkill must be allowed to show themselves, as must the valve handle and the prickly pears. True sight demands that we touch the surface of the world as it is. But, in the interim, there are times when the eye requires a swell of fog and the generosity of its cloak.

Ireland in the 1980s needed a cloak. Violence in the North. Hunger strikes. Thatcher and Reagan. The hands of church and state resting heavy upon the bodies of women. An ocean away, my neighborhood had its own bleakness. Mothers went to Corpus Christi Church, lines of children trailing behind them as they looked to Saint Joseph and the gospel writers but most of all to the sweet face of Mary. What better remedy to drudgery than hope? What better balm for hard times than possibility?

Still, it's tough to know what to make of a throng of moving statues. A smiling statue, while wondrous, isn't exactly a heavy hitter as far as miracles are concerned. Of what consequence a blinking concrete figure? Are we such beggars – accepting a nod as a stand-in for meaningful movement, allowing a momentary flutter of eyes in place of a living breathing human being stepping into the drizzle to spread a mantle over a suffering child?

Or maybe a moving statue is not so minor a miracle after all – and the opening of the eyes not such a small act. We open and close them thousands of times a day, so that we have no choice but to take looking for granted. But there is no more perfect consecration than attention. We elevate what we behold. Seeing is a chrism, a way of anointing, the closest we come to being priests.

A friend from Cork took me to Ballinspittle a few summers back. She generously gave a tour of the coast, driving us to a fort, guiding us past the brightly painted houses of Kinsale and the beach where tall grasses sprout from dunes and families parked in campers for their holidays, and finally to the grotto at Ballinspittle where we sat on a roadside bench painted blue, looking at Mary beneath a bower of greenery, a stone's throw from a kneeling plaster Bernadette caught in perpetual supplication.

I was in high school back when the statue was said to open her eyes – the same age Ann Lovett would have been if she'd survived giving birth in the frozen grotto. 1985. Back then all I knew about Ireland besides U2 songs were the Troubles of the North, which were added to the litany of intentions every week at Mass.

We sat there. Two women. Both working at our local universities. Both with time for the reading of books and the pursuing of thoughts. Different from each other, yes, but light years removed from our mothers with their shrines and rosaries and stubborn insistence on mystery and faith. The hillside was lush with ferns and gorse, and birds sounded in the fields around us.

Not far away, the sea. To our backs, a few kilometers along the peninsula, the Old Head of Kinsale. We'd stopped there earlier, walking up the cliff to a view of rushing water and birds soaring in coves below. The same reverence was present as we looked up the hillside toward the Virgin, and it seemed to me there was something of our mothers in us after all. Were we acting out a devotion pressed upon us by our pasts or beholding the statue with clear vision – seeing beyond her prescribed proportions and obedient virginity to something else?

It was women and girls who'd most often reported seeing the statues move. Women and girls who filed onto buses for visits to the shrines. Women and girls who said rosaries when their knees ached, when the rent was due, and their invocations to man fell upon unyielding ears.

We sat there at Ballinspittle, a breeze fluttering the fuchsia and roses. Now and then a car passed. The driver might look up to the figure cast in plaster, but would he see what we did? A woman crowning a hilltop. Haloed in light, a length of sky tied around her waist – a woman who appeared locked safely into place, her bare feet tipping imperceptibly away from her stone base, inching ever so slowly toward movement.

SEARCH FOR THE VIRGIN, PART IV

Pittsburgh

The movement of statues is not as unusual as people might expect.

Used Church Items specializes in the acquisition and sale of devotional items from pre–Vatican II worship sites. When I found their website and emailed one of the proprietors to ask if I could visit their Pittsburgh warehouse, Mike Osella generously obliged.

I exit the interstate south of Pittsburgh and wind past fields edged with chicory and Queen Anne's lace and gas stations selling bait. In town I pass an American Legion post, then turn off the main strip into an area of warehouses, and park near an old building quietly succumbing to vines.

Life-size statues crowd together like concertgoers just inside the warehouse doors. Every imaginable saint appears to be represented, in every imaginable form.

"Saint Joseph is our biggest seller," Mike says. Their customers are churches looking for replacement fixtures, seminarians wanting quality chalices, sisters seeking a crèche for the motherhouse. An enormous Christ the King awaits shipment to Singapore for use in a procession. Just days before my visit a pair of A-list celebrities had toured the warehouse with an eye toward creating a private chapel. But not everyone they sell to is religious. Their items appear on film sets and television backdrops.

"You've seen our stuff in movies and miniseries," Mike says, and lists familiar titles.

Mike's father began collecting when the changes of Vatican II led to items associated with the traditional Latin Mass falling out of favor. A Catholic and an antique dealer, Jason Osella tried to salvage pieces he recognized as valuable or finely wrought. He bought and stored the objects wherever he could, which meant statues often shared their home. "It must have been fun to bring friends over," I joke, and Mike laughs. "Actually, it was."

Statues are the tip of the iceberg. Shelves teem with censers and sacristy bells. A vestment room houses hundreds of brocaded chasubles and embroidered stoles. The second floor holds sets of chandeliers and stations of the cross. There are baptismal fonts and kneelers, canopies and paintings, pulpits and croziers, altar crosses and panels of stained glass.

Downstairs a room is filled with gold-plated vessels. Glass cases reflect the sheen of polished chalices; monstrances gleam like little suns. I spin around, giddy and stunned. The room leaks so much light, all of western Pennsylvania seems to shine.

The Osellas are generous with their time, especially since, despite my attempts to explain, none of us quite understands why I've come. *I'm interested in what happens to devotional items when churches close*, I'd written in my email. But not everything ends up in a warehouse to be repaired and readied for resale. Some objects are transferred locally. Others are sold to outside dioceses, parishioners, and the general public. Still others remain locked in closets and vestries, are melted down, or are altogether discarded. In an era of closed churches, things pile up. Remaining parishes can only absorb so much.

But we humans get attached. Against all reason and logic, devotion becomes entwined with the spaces in which it is enacted and the objects that help to inspire and focus it. Our places and people come and go so quickly we want to hold onto what remains. A mother's ring, a grandfather's desk – even an old plaster statue – such things come to matter more when so little of the past is salvageable.

I scan the warehouse one last time. Though I know better, I stare into the swarm of faces to see if any of the Blessed Mothers are mine. The end of summer is drawing near. I'll be leaving for my teaching job in Virginia soon. We go back and forth from Rochester to Richmond, my husband and I, maintaining a long-distance marriage during the semesters, making time together rare. Even on long weekends back in Rochester there will be no time to look for my lost Lady. The search will have to wait until I come north over the holidays.

"I'd like to buy something," I say to Mike as I get ready to leave. I look through a cabinet of statuettes and settle on a foot-high Saint Joseph the Worker holding a pitcher and loaf of bread, the paint of his apron and right hand chipped.

"This one," I say, but Mike won't hear of my paying and makes a gift of the statue, which I swaddle in soft cloth and lay on his side for the long drive home.

7

Litany for a Dying Church

"Just a building," a sensible person says, and even as I trace
patterns where the floorboards are worn from years of people
shuffling in and out of pews, I have to concede the point.
 Just a building, true. But think of all it's held.
 Babies soft as new flowers wriggling in godparents' arms.
Legions of nervous brides. Girls tittering in Communion dresses,
boys in pressed suits and slicked-back hair. Holy water like ice
upon the forehead on January mornings. Third graders from the
school across the way, the one who's forgotten her homework
and sweats through the Confiteor. *Through my fault, through my
fault, through my most grievous fault.* The overworked principal
and the sisters with their black and white habits. The bingo
caller with his Alabama accent down in the hall. The man in
the last pew praying as if his life depends on it. Those whose
lives do depend on it. The bustle of clerics and the housekeeper
who hums to keep from thinking of her sore feet as she makes
up their beds. The silk chasubles and velvet-cushioned seats.
Confessions murmured through the screen. *Bless me, Father.*
All that's said and heard and washed away. All that remains
locked inside the body's tender vault. A century of spaghetti
dinners and raffle tickets and three-tiered cakes. Plate upon
endless potluck plate of ambrosia salad and chicken French.
The bloom of Saint Anthony's face, his sheaf of plaster lilies,
the way he holds the Child year after year without ever buckling
at the knee. The click of rosaries and creak of kneelers. The

priest who left for love. The one who stayed for the same. Those who ignore each other during the Sign of Peace and those who don't and the various signs of peace themselves: smiles and waves and barely perceptible nods; hands finding each other; kisses breathed onto cheeks; the bachelor touched once a week his entire life. A flurry of genuflections and breast-beatings and crossings. *In nomine Patris et Filii et Spiritus Sancti.* One hundred fifteen years of accumulated motion. Enough to stir up a minor hurricane.

If everyone on earth spit at the same time, we'd all drown, my friend Angie once announced on the way to Mass. My head went so soggy with the prospect and sheer calculations it's taken four decades and a return to our old sanctuary to formulate a response: *If everyone who ever set foot in this church sang a psalm at the same time, our hearts would become birds and fly straight into each other's hands.*

8

Feast of Saint Blaise

One summer it became the thing to do to have your house blessed. First one mother on the street asked the priest to come and bless her house, then the next. Soon Father Jim was sprinkling holy water inside half the living rooms on the tiny dead end, including ours. This is not so unusual. Think of any object or occasion that can matter to a person and some Catholic somewhere has had it blessed. And while I'm not the sort to seek them out, neither am I inclined to turn a good blessing away.

I accepted, for instance, the oversized medal of Our Lady of Guadalupe my friend Mary offered the last time I visited (though I did, in all honesty, decline the Padre Pio pendant). I said yes on Epiphany when parishioners were handed bits of holy chalk with which to inscribe blessings upon our homes. Last summer I waited in line to enter the benediction booth outside the gift shop at the shrine at Beaupré and crossed myself as the priest on shift consecrated a Pope Francis prayer card. And, of course, we are officially blessed each and every week at church – but somehow, in all these years, I'd never had my throat blessed.

The ritual of throat blessings has been practiced on the Feast of Saint Blaise for centuries, but my post–Vatican II parish avoided such showy traditions, or – because the blessings occurred in early February – my family never managed the walk to church in the deep freeze. Either way, I'd never partaken. When I saw a nearby church advertising the blessings this year, it seemed the right time. *I'm prone to sore throats*, I thought, *so why not?*

If I were in Rome on February 3, I could go to the Church of San Carlo ai Catinari and be blessed with a relic of the saint encased in a crystal ring. In Croatia I might join a procession through the center of Dubrovnik with banners and brass bands and legions of white doves, followed by Mass and *grličanje* (throat blessings) at the Church of St. Blaise. But I'm in my hometown of Rochester, New York, where, as in most places, the Blessing of the Throats is bestowed with two candles bound by a specially made candelabrum.

Because the blessings are not offered in every parish, I drive to a neighboring church and stand in line before a priest who, with his round face, resembles an uncle who worked at the Genesee Brewery and nipped occasionally from the vats. The priest sets the vee of crossed candles against our necks and blesses us, one at a time. He speaks words from *The Book of Blessings*, which includes prayers for boats and fishing gear, fields and flocks, libraries and confessional booths. Today it's throats. The red-faced priest invokes the blessing on all who come before him. With about sixty or so people in line, I wonder about the effect of the ritual on his own throat:

By the intercession of Saint Blaise, bishop and martyr, he says. *May God deliver you from every disease of the throat.*

Unlike in the old days, the candles are not lit – which is fortunate, given how cold the day and the profusion of scarves and woolen collars. Back in my pew I feel a bit more connected to others around me by virtue of our joint participation in the quirky custom. When Mass ends I step from the church to my car and make my way downtown to a rally that also happens to be planned for today.

I hardly go to rallies anymore. In my early twenties I marched and made signs and chanted until my throat was raw. I wrote letters, sat in, was even once arrested. But I'd grown mild over the years and convinced that all that protesting had fallen primarily into my own ears. I turned my bids for peace inward, which suited my tendency toward introversion just fine. But by February of last year everything had changed. Days after his inauguration, the new president had issued orders restricting immigration and sanctioning cities offering sanctuary. When I saw the rally advertised, I knew I had to go.

My face freezes into a mask as I walk toward Rochester City Hall. Hats and gloves are nothing against the cut of air. Still, hundreds have gathered on the steps and in the streets surrounding the building, holding signs and standing together in the bitter cold. I bring my hand to my throat and think of Blaise. A physician from an upper-class Christian family before being elected bishop, he was well loved and martyred in 316. Little else is known of Blaise's life. When the saint is remembered at all, it's for the miracle attributed to him upon his arrest.

Persecution against Christians had been officially abolished with the Edict of Milan three years before, but Licinius in the East did not always abide by the agreement reached with his co-emperor and frequent enemy, Constantine, in the West. Licinius's latest assault, in fact, targeted bishops, which put a bounty on Blaise's head and sent him hiding in the mountains near Sebaste.

It's said that animals were drawn to the gentle bishop. Like Saint Francis of Assisi who would follow, Blaise had a special way with wild creatures. He was kind, talking to animals as he would people and tending those with wounds. When a group of hunters tracked the animals to his cave and discovered Blaise, they knew they'd struck gold. They seized the bishop, leading him down from the mountain, marching him past scrub pine and ledges of volcanic rock. How shocked the party must have been when a woman came running over and threw herself into their path. "Help," she sobbed to the bishop, face contorted with pain, dark hair matted with tears and dirt. In her arms a child struggled for breath. The boy had a fish bone lodged in his throat and the mother was so desperate to save him that the sight of men with drawn swords did not deter her. And though he was clearly in the middle of his own crisis, according to legend Blaise stopped and made the sign of the cross upon the boy, dislodging the bone and linking the bishop forever with ailments of the throat.

Some versions of Blaise's story say the mother brought her child to his prison cell. Others have Blaise touching a candle to the neck of one of his guards to relieve his chronic pain. And how did Blaise happen to have candles? He'd received them from a woman whose pig he'd rescued from the mouth of a wolf. She'd been distraught at the loss of her animal, but when Blaise asked the wolf to release the pig from the snare of his teeth, the wolf kindly obliged. In gratitude the woman brought Blaise a share of bread and two candles to light his cell.

As far as hagiographies go, it's a good one. Word of Blaise's goodness spread. He was honored first by the Eastern church and eventually by the West. In the Middle Ages he was included as one of Fourteen Holy Helpers during the years of the Black Death. His name was invoked alongside saints such as Denis (for headaches), Barbara (for fever), and Elmo (for abdominal troubles). A set of curative superheroes. People petitioned the Helpers in their darkest days, when families huddled around sickbeds and such invocations provided their only hope.

At the rally I pull my collar over my neck and wonder what Blaise would think of throat blessings, if I could pull him from ancient Armenia to the present day. I'm guessing he'd smile and find the tradition sweet. He was a doctor, after all, and who could find fault with any blessing bestowed upon the body?

But it would not be lost on him – the silence, our silence – on the very principles Christianity was founded (love of neighbor, care for the poor, welcoming all). And though he might be too polite to mention it, our acquiescence would stand in stark contrast to his own actions as he was hauled off to jail. Nobody would have blamed him if, in this moment of profound distress – probably the greatest of his life – he'd not seen the crying woman or heard the child's labored breath. The lowest of the low – a woman and child – and he, a bishop on his way to certain death. But he did see her crouching there. He did hear the boy's wheezing and forgot his own trouble long enough to reach out his hand. And later, when he was dragged before the governor, Blaise had only to renounce his beliefs to stop the horrors inflicted upon him. Just a word to save his own neck. But he refused. Even as he was tortured and executed. How tame our religion would seem to him, I fear, how close to the trappings of the empire whose politicians had hauled him off to jail.

It seems no accident that his most famous act – the one we still honor him for after nearly two thousand years – involves unsticking a throat. He healed the boy's breathing, yes. But the throat is made for more than breath.

I look around at the faces at the rally, mittened hands holding signs, breath making little clouds as we chant, and think again of the blessing at church. How quiet we'd been. How easily we'd slipped from our pews back to our cars and the various pulls of our lives. We'd remembered Blaise on his feast day, yes, invoking his name against strep and laryngitis and maladies of the throat, but Blaise's faith was a wild pulsing force. When had we remade his legacy into a quaint custom and relegated one of our most radical saints to the role of a sacred cough drop?

Which is not to say that I object to the blessing. I understand better why the mothers on our street had their houses blessed that summer so long ago. Once touched by holy water and prayers, our plaid couches and cracked linoleum floors seemed to shine for a time. I've become more open to blessings and may even stand before a priest again next year.

But attending a protest at city hall on the Feast of Saint Blaise reminded me of the obligation of speech in times of darkness and of the metaphorical fish bone lodged in my own throat – a throat all the more blessed by gathering with others in the frigid chapel of evening and calling out for what I knew to be true and right.

9

Devil's Advocate

Sister Lilian's body was found near the confessional. Father Weinmann was collapsed beside her but still breathing. The curtain of smoke had tricked them into thinking they'd reached the exit, but instead of opening a door onto the cold afternoon, they'd found only a small booth divided by a screen, a seat on one side and kneeler on the other. Flames made easy work of the church. The fire traveled from apse to ceiling, caught along the aisles, and swallowed the sanctuary with smoke.

Earlier in the day the snow had changed to drizzle, but had cleared enough by noon to allow the children outside for recess. Rochester, New York. Situated on Lake Ontario's southern shore, the city was battered by winds coming south from Canada and east from Buffalo. Some days the kids slipped into the church to get warm. They were only outside a few minutes that February day in 1967 when a fourth grader told a boy on safety patrol that kids were playing inside the church. By the time the older boy opened the door, the altar was engulfed in flames. He rushed out and sounded the alarm. Everything quickened in his wake. Priests ran from the rectory without cassocks. Nuns tumbled from the school in dark veils. They ushered children into lines, led them to a nearby side street, and tried to distract them from the burning church. Impossible, of course. Sirens tore into the hollows of their ears. Smoke stung the insides of their noses. "Don't look back," the sisters said. The children would have known the story of Lot's wife, but what is a pillar of salt compared to flames blooming like an out-of-season rose?

Built as a mission in an Italian neighborhood in the northeast section of the city, the one-story church was constructed entirely of wood. The air pulsed and cracked as flames licked the planks clean and smoke gushed from the bell tower in tremendous plumes.

Father Weinmann entered the church first. He'd run outside without shoes and rushed into the burning sanctuary to save the Blessed Sacrament. The seventy-seven-year-old priest struggled at the altar – the lock to the tabernacle would not give or he was blinded by smoke. Either way he attempted to drag the entire tabernacle to safety, but the bulk of the brass box impeded his progress.

Nothing impeded Sister Lilian Marie McLaughlin. After calling the fire department the second grade teacher removed her veil, swallowed a final breath of cool air, and pushed in through the side door.

A photograph in the next day's paper shows four men bending into the stretcher holding Sister Lilian's body. The men lift together, snow piled at their feet. The faces of onlookers are woven like ghosts into the backdrop. The nun had celebrated her twenty-sixth birthday only two days before, blowing out candles and eating cake, but by the time snow descended on the burnt church that night, the teacher had moved from ordinary human being to a model of self-sacrifice. Father Weinmann would live another two days, but Sister Lilian died on the scene and was declared a martyr by Rochester bishop Fulton Sheen, who said she *gave her life in helping Father Weinmann save the Blessed Sacrament from fire. Greater love than this no woman hath.*

Saint Philip Neri was not far from where my family lived. Just a few streets to the north and it would have been my mother's church, Father Weinmann her priest, and Sister Lilian her children's teacher. Hers would have been one of the telephones ringing off the hook back in the winter of 1967, women gossiping about the tragic loss of life, the horror of the flames, and how close to them their children had been. My mother, who'd just turned twenty-seven, would have nodded, thinking perhaps of how close she was to Sister Lilian's age.

But it happened that she lived a fraction to the south and east and went to Mass at Corpus Christi. Even if she'd attended St. Philip Neri, her phone might not have rung off the hook or she might not have answered, for there was nothing traditional about my mother. She was, in fact, more likely to be the source of gossip than its recipient. But some Sundays, when it was not too cold to walk the mile or so over the railroad bridge to church, my mother rounded up her children and told them to brush their teeth while she stared out the window and enjoyed the last few months before her stomach blossomed again into a globe. My mother's body was not yet busy with me, but she'd already met the man who would kick things off. Eventually she'd learn he was married. Later she'd say she was blindsided. In time there would be insinuations of sin and martyrdom – but in the winter of 1967 there was only snow and fire, and when I came into the world a year later the earth was already scorched where the little church once stood.

For Catholics sainthood is more than a question of goodness. Petitions must be made. Miracles must be verified. Official examinations of the candidate's actions, attitudes, and influence must be undertaken.

The Congregation for the Causes of Saints oversees the process as candidates rise from local petitions to Vatican review and move along the path from Servant of God to Venerable to Blessed (beatification). The final designation of Saint must be conferred by the Pope, and pontiffs have differed greatly in their approach. Some cases are fast-tracked while others linger. Miracles are tough to document. There are wars to contend with, politics to consider. Famine. Death. Petitions accidentally shuffled into back drawers. The candidacy for a group of men martyred at Otranto, Italy, in 1480, for instance, began sixty years after their deaths in 1539. They were beatified more than two hundred years later, in 1771, but would not be canonized for another two and half centuries, in 2013.

To safeguard the rigor of the process, the Church employed an official skeptic. The *advocatus diaboli* (devil's advocate) was trained in canon law and charged by the Vatican to argue against cases for sainthood. Known formally as the *promotor fidei* (promoter of the faith), the devil's advocate was established about the time Protestants began to rebel against Church excesses, which motivated Rome to clean up its act to ensure that those it sainted were deserving of such a title. The devil's advocate scrutinized each case, cross-examined witnesses, challenged miracles, and interrogated the holiness of the proposed saint's life.

His primary adversary was *advocatus Dei* (God's advocate), who supported canonization. The two men battled – one for, one against – taking every opportunity to promote their cause. If God's advocate slept in or missed his morning coffee, the case might go to the devil and we'd miss out on a saint. If the devil's advocate was distracted by a minor flirtation or indigestion from a seafood stew, he might not argue as vehemently and let a sinner slip past – so it happened that sinners were occasionally sainted and saints were sometimes overlooked.

Bishop Sheen is himself a candidate for sainthood.

Perhaps the most popular American Catholic until JFK, from 1930 to 1950 Sheen enjoyed an audience of millions for his *Catholic Hour* on radio. When television came along, even more tuned in to see him on the screen. In his cape and red silk zucchetto, the bishop referred to his viewers as *friends* and chose a few of the thousands of daily letters he received to read on the air, responding to each with a barrage of corny jokes. Backed by bookcases and a chalkboard on which he scribbled key concepts on such wide-ranging topics as "How to Psycho-analyze Yourself" and "False Compassion" and "Our Lady of Fatima," Sheen presented his lessons as the elegant and intense professor he must have been in his Catholic University days. Even children were charmed and sent in their allowances to aid the needy via missions Sheen undertook as head of the Society for the Propagation of the Faith.

His assignment to Rochester in late 1966 resulted from trouble with Cardinal Spellman in New York. It's said the cardinal wanted access to donations that skyrocketed during Sheen's tenure. When Sheen refused he was backed by Rome, but the cardinal retaliated – using his political muscle to remove Sheen from committee appointments, force him off the air, and render him increasingly unwelcome in New York City churches. Rochester was so far north it was practically Canada, and Sheen's three-hundred-mile move west amounted to exile.

Sheen's star did not shine as brightly in the upstate diocese. Beleaguered by local squabbles and the massive upheaval following Vatican II, the seventy-four-year-old bishop resigned after three years, but oversaw the diocese long enough to preside at confirmations, ordinations, and funerals – including those of the victims of the St. Philip Neri fire. Sheen eulogized Father Weinmann as *a martyred priest on behalf of his Blessed Lord*, and proclaimed Sister Lilian *a modern saint in a time when we are losing faith*.

As for his own sainthood, twenty years after Sheen's death the petition for canonization was opened by the bishop of his home diocese in Peoria. Ten years later the cause was approved by Rome. Declared to have lived a life of heroic virtue, Sheen was given the title *Venerable*. A miracle was found. Another suggested. But the case was suspended in 2014 when the Archdiocese of New York – where Sheen has been interred at St. Patrick's Cathedral since 1979 – refused to send his remains to Peoria for examination and the taking of relics, both required for canonization. The case is now being waged in court, with those in

Peoria fighting for Sheen's body's and those in New York refusing to part with it, leaving the former Bishop of Rochester caught somewhere between Servant of God and Blessed.

Sainthood was not so formal in the early days. Eventually Rome would embrace Christianity and a clerical hierarchy would emerge outfitted in the trappings of the empire. Churches would move from catacombs and homes to sumptuous public buildings. Bishops, and eventually popes, would decide who was deemed *sanctus* (holy) and who was not.

But in the first few centuries Christians had simply recognized holiness when they saw it. Martyrs were the original saints. Their stories flourished. Accounts were filled with rebellion, perseverance, and wonder. Agnes, for instance, whose beauty was said to enflame men, but who held as fast to her virginity as she did to her faith. When she was dragged through the streets of Rome, her hair grew and covered her naked body with its tresses. When they tried to rape her, her assailants were struck blind. When they tied her to a stake, the fire would not catch. Even after a soldier drew his sword and her murder finally took, Agnes did not stay put, appearing fifty years later to Lucy of Sicily, another beauty similarly martyred for her faith.

Saints existed for every virtue, region, and mood. For musical devotion: Cecilia, who, even on her wedding day sang in her heart only to God. For tragic beauty: Sebastian, bound to a tree and shot with arrows. For strong women: Thecla, who shaved her head and donned men's clothes so her voice would be heard. For love: old Valentine himself, upon whose life no one seems to agree, except that he was martyred in the third century, and a skull marked with his name is crowned with flowers in the *Basilica di Santa Maria* in Rome.

The St. Philip Neri fire came less than a week after Valentine's Day. Construction paper hearts would have been taped to the windows of elementary schools all over the city. In fact, a small fire had been found in the church on Valentine's Day. Faulty wiring, people said. It was easily contained and the scent masked with lemon oil for weekend Masses. There'd been other incidents – singed paper, burnt altar cloth – but nobody thought much of them until the fatal fire on February 20 when, like the accounts of the early saints, the story of Father Weinmann running into the burning sanctuary with Sister Lilian at his heels flourished, buzzing over telephone wires and during coffee hours after Mass. *Eucharistic Martyrs*, they were called. Sister Lilian grew lovelier with each telling. How magnificent her heart. How obedient and humble she was to aid the priest in his sacred task. In an era of social and religious upheaval, it's not surprising many found such devotion inspiring – even comforting, perhaps.

The only problem is that Sister Lilian doesn't seem to have followed Father Weinmann into the church, but instead entered of her own accord. Those who knew her best say the teacher ran into the burning building to be sure it was clear of children. A report of kids playing inside is what alerted the safety patrol to the fire, after all. *Children in the church.* The words would have ricocheted in the air. By the time Sister Lilian ran inside, the smoke would have been so thick she'd have barely been able to see her own hands. She'd have searched the small sanctuary, feeling her way past pews, bending beneath them to check for small bodies. But there were no children. No one was inside, in fact, except for Father Weinmann struggling at the altar. Sister Lilian saw him there and turned to help the elderly priest instead of escaping the fire. An act of bravery, no doubt. An instance of utter selflessness, certainly. A martyr, yes – a eucharistic martyr even – but only if we allow that the tabernacle she sought to safeguard was not a brass box. Both priest and nun heard the word "fire" and thought immediately of the Body of Christ – but where an image of the ciborium flashed before Father Weinmann, Sister Lilian seems to have seen the golden oval of a child's face.

Declarations of sainthood are relatively rare, but the designation became more common in 1983 when Pope John Paul II greatly reduced the adversarial nature of the proceedings. The role of the devil's advocate was abandoned, and the floodgates opened. John Paul canonized 482 new saints and beatified 1,338 – more than all the popes before him combined. His decision to streamline the process led to concern that too many saints were slipping by, with some even calling the Vatican a "saint factory." The Church retightened the guidelines in 2008, but Pope Francis has already surpassed John Paul II's numbers with his 2013 canonization of all 813 martyrs of Otranto.

But what does it really mean, to be sainted by the Church? Apart from an entry in the canon? What can it matter to Lucy or Agnes what anyone calls them once they're gone? What can it matter to Sister Lilian – whose flat marker in the nuns' section at Holy Sepulchre Cemetery is dwarfed by the headstones in the priests' section where Father Weinmann lies? Such distinctions matter most to those needing models of courage and grace as we make our way through difficult days. Perhaps that's why we continue to assign status even in death – erecting finer monuments to some than others, clinging to the last to our need to categorize and rank. Only the bones are free of such entanglements. They let go of their salt and marrow and sink into the earth until it's impossible to parse sinner from saint.

In early March the same fourth grader whose report of children playing in the church had alerted others to the blaze was caught setting a small fire in the school basement. The official cause of the St. Philip Neri fire was faulty wiring, but when confronted by the principal the ten-year-old admitted to playing with matches, to using a taper to light curtains and altar linens and then staying around to watch them burn. The local paper reported the story, providing the boy's age, details about the fire, and the fact that he was studying to be an altar boy. But after one article the story disappeared, so that in the years that followed, when the fire was remembered, faulty wiring was most often claimed as its cause.

A saint, that principal, to let the boy go. Or maybe it wasn't her choice. Perhaps she thought of her lost sister, bit a bottom lip, and recommended he be turned in. The new pastor may have advocated for the boy. Or Bishop Sheen himself. Or the group of them together. *Two lives have been lost already*, someone would have said. *Why add a third?*

It was Lent. Ashes would have been pressed upon the boy's forehead days before the fire. He'd have been given his Self-Denial Folder with the image of the crucified Christ on its cover and encouraged to collect nickels and dimes for the diocese in the inside slots. Did they look into his face, that group of adults? Did anyone wonder if the boy had acted out of some hidden pain, attempting to inflict what burned inside him onto the outside world? What chance did whatever troubled the child stand of being spoken of openly in 1967?

I see them there – father and son, priest and nun, celebrated bishop in his newly assigned exile – each of them staggering under the weight of their losses, barely able to look each other in the eye. The father waves his hands as he speaks. The boy's head hangs nearly to the floor. The principal sets a hand on his arm. The bishop in his study scribbles thoughts on redemption and grace while trying without success to keep images of St. Patrick's Cathedral at bay. How effortlessly they rise before me. How easy it is to see them as collectively culpable as it is to imagine them a roomful of saints.

Had the fire raged a year later, I'd have breathed in the char and seen the neighborhood darken through the slits of my infant eyes. Just a year later, but the world had remade itself by then. Priests had traded in their cassocks for black uniform pants. Sisters had removed their wimples and veils. A lifetime away, 1967 and St. Philip Neri. But in certain moments I feel closer to the lost church and to my mother in her Leighton Avenue kitchen than I do my own life.

When I'm back in Rochester, I drive down the streets where they once sat and stood and stretched into patches of sun: my father, Father Weinmann, the boy's parents. I think of Bishop Sheen, his body now trapped in the place where he'd once been so cruelly shut out. I think of Sister Lilian laughing as she blows out twenty-six candles. I think of the boy with a pack of matches, the sulfur scent of his fingertips, and the way some fires start. I think of my mother in South Texas, alone after all these years, tracking a bird from her window and trying her best to paint a red hibiscus. I think of myself shadowing ghosts and scouring the wreckage. I think of us – all of us – and the push and pull of human flesh.

It's not easy to become a saint, but some say that's who we are.

Father Bob starts Sunday Mass by saying, *God morning, Saints*.

And while the changing of *good* to *god* is familiar – a reversal of what I've done in my head since I was a kid – it's strange to hear it spoken aloud and nearly too punlike for church. But how quickly I've grown used to it. How I'd miss it if he ever stopped. How I'd mourn the loss of his looking up and out into the congregation – no matter how we slump in the pews, how lackluster our singing, or how impervious we appear to his words – before anything else, the priest stands at the altar, looks into our faces, and calls out:

God morning, saints.

Good morning, Father, we say, and this is the beginning of church.

SEARCH FOR THE VIRGIN, PART V

Buffalo

The scrape of a snowplow interrupts Perry Como's smooth baritone on the twenty-four-hour Christmas station. Rock salt spins from the back of utility trucks as traffic crawls along Route 33 West. "Silver Bells," I sing along while watching snow hit the windshield and wondering for the thousandth time what I'm doing in Buffalo.

When my visits to churches on the weekends surrounding Thanksgiving led me no closer to my blue-mantled Lady, I planned a week in Buffalo during my holiday break. I wouldn't be able to get to most parishes – even with massive closures a decade ago, the city still teems with so many churches that their towers and domes define the landscape. In western New York Catholic churches sit like jewel boxes in working-class neighborhoods, their spires soaring above pizza places and bowling alleys. As kids we walked by the neighborhood bar, a fish market, and several bodegas to get there. I loved the Mass, yes, but I also went because it was the prettiest place I knew, and ours was a rather ordinary church.

If I'd grown up near St. Louis Church in Buffalo, someone would have had to pry me from the pew. A reservoir of mosaics and high-flung arches – enormous panels of stained glass soak the sanctuary with light. The only thing more astounding than its interior is how many other churches are similarly dazzling. St. Mary in Medina. Holy Family in Albion. St. Michael in Rochester. Even run-of-the-mill city churches often feature exquisitely carved altars, handcrafted tabernacles, rose windows, and expansive celestial murals. And, in every one, a place of honor for the Blessed Mother. More than any other feature, the presence of the Virgin Mary symbolizes the identity of a Catholic church.

Images of Mary vary according to the communities and churches themselves. Our Lady of Czestochowa is popular in the Polish parishes of Buffalo, for instance, while the Madonna della Libera can be found at St. Anthony of Padua, where Masses are still celebrated in Italian. A 1,600-pound marble Our Lady of Victory soars from the altar of Father Baker's lavish Lackawanna basilica, while a simple wood-carved Our Lady of Hope complements the welcoming west side parish of the same name. The Virgin in the Seneca Street shrine, commissioned by a neighborhood barber after a 1950s apparition, is a midcentury vision in her belted day dress and sweep of unbound hair.

I make the rounds, visiting old parishes, newly formed clusters, and suburban sites that might have added a chapel in the past decade. In the evenings I attend holiday concerts and Advent services, but rely on daily Mass for the bulk of my detective work. I rise for a 7:00 a.m. Mass in one church, followed by an 8:15 at another, and later a 12:05. I slip in and out of sanctuaries, lighting a candle and sitting a minute. The Virgin at St. Katharine Drexel has a cloak so blue I have to check several times to be sure she's not mine, but despite the occasional similarity to her, the Prince Street Virgin is nowhere to be found.

It's undoubtedly foolish – this driving all over Buffalo in winter looking for a statue. I slide along icy roads during the day and toss and turn at night, questioning my use of time and resources and doubting myself every step of the way. But I also love it. The churches are gorgeous, each with its unique history and human stories. When else would I have an excuse to visit so many? How much longer will they be around?

Still, by week's end, I am no closer to finding her.

I imagine posting "MISSING STATUE" signs on utility poles all over Buffalo. Instead, I do the modern equivalent and post on Facebook. I upload photos and ask friends to ask friends if they've seen her. When the Diocese of Buffalo shares my post, people are friendly and interested but no one knows a thing. What now? I wonder. Is it time to give up? Probably. Instead, I begin to email those parishes I could not visit a few days before Christmas – sending out lost-statue missives during the busiest time of the year.

It's the height of the holiday season with my family and friends sixty miles away. I cannot stay in Buffalo forever. I eat cut-out cookies and shop on Elmwood Avenue but, when I can delay no more, pack up my car to head home. On my way to the thruway I decide to peek into one last church. Just one more, I tell myself. The city's cathedral, St. Joseph's, has an impressive collection of Marian images and is not likely to harbor the humble Rochester Virgin, but I'm on a sugar high and past the point of reason, so I angle my car into a half-plowed spot. Once inside I rush past Saint Anthony and nearly trip over my own feet trying to reach the statue of a female saint I'd seen as I walked in. Thérèse of Lisieux. The crucifix and roses give her away. I let out a sigh and think of my car probably getting ticketed about now. And just as I turn around and prepare to push on, I realize I'm frowning. Before the exquisite image of a saint. I stop and look around. Light filters through enormous panels of stained glass. The ceilings are soaring and white. Freshly cut evergreens are stacked just inside the doors, dozens of trees awaiting placement on the altar for Christmas Eve. The scent of balsam floods the cathedral and refreshes every last part of me as I close my eyes and breathe it in.

Look what you almost missed, I say to myself. *Am I so caught up in this impossible quest I'm willing to miss out on the beauty smack-dab in front of my face?*

I look around one last time, breathing in the clean scent.

Okay, I say. *Clearly, it's time to move on.*

10

Act of Contrition

I'd had sin on my mind weeks before arriving in Louisiana. Months, in fact. My return to church had not been without bumps, but I'd set aside doubt and allowed myself to rediscover the beauty of Catholic tradition – except for confession, which seemed to me the black sheep in the family of sacraments. Even in my churchiest days I'd never fully appreciated it. This makes me somewhat ashamed but fairly typical. Most Catholics don't go to confession. Despite programs at the diocesan level, billboard campaigns, and mobile apps to help bolster the sacrament, only 3% of Catholics report confessing at least once a month, with many going once a year, but even more never going at all. What is it about confession that seems so woefully out of date, I wondered even as I avoided it, and what do we lose as we back away?

I reread my favorite scene in *Portrait of the Artist as a Young Man*. The young Stephen Dedalus is knee-deep in sin for a sizeable chunk of the novel and tormented by hellish fear, but once he has confessed he practically floats from the booth, overwhelmed by a sudden and pulsing connection to the larger world. *How simple and beautiful was life after all!* Stephen thinks, experiencing one of those luminous interludes we occasionally fall into when the circumstances rightly align – a heightened awareness, a certain angle of light, the small and the superficial held momentarily at bay. Hadn't my hunger for such moments help propel me back to church?

I'm sure I celebrated First Penance, though I struggle to recall it – and *celebrate* isn't the verb I'd have used. I stood in line during group services or youth retreats, bowed my head, and repeated the few canned sins I expected a priest might like to hear (*I'd lied. I'd sworn. I'd fought with my sisters.*). True, but hardly the most serious blockages along my spiritual path. Ours was a priest who preached love in place of fear. I'd never heard a word of condemnation, and *sin* was never a meaningful part of my vocabulary. The word was batted about, of course, but like *hallowed* and *apostolic* it was too old-fashioned and laden a concept to cling to, like trying to spin cartwheels with cast iron skillets lining the pockets of your pants.

Fast-forward thirty years. I sat listening as our priest encouraged confession during Lent and Advent or one of the summer programs. Maybe, I'd think. But when the time came I'd be out of town. I'll go eventually, I told myself. It went that way for months, the liturgical calendar moving from Christmas to Easter and back again to Ordinary Time. I didn't go to confession, but neither did it leave me be.

Which is why I've come to southern Louisiana. I want to meet the priest who's converted an old ambulance into a mobile confessional – a Spiritual Care Unit, Father Champagne calls it – complete with kneeler and curtain, holy water, and prayer cards. Father Michael Champagne drives the confessional throughout Cajun Country, parking outside restaurants and health clubs, visiting nursing homes and community festivals. He started the project a few years ago, heeding Pope Francis's call to be more active in bringing people back to church. If the Church was a field hospital, as the pontiff had suggested, Father Champagne took the analogy literally with his ambulance. The Spiritual Care Unit has traveled thousands of miles and played host to thousands of confessions. When I read about the project I reached out to Father Champagne, who invited me to visit. Besides an interest in his commitment to the sacrament, I suppose I'm hoping that the Spiritual Care Unit will be so out of the ordinary I'll fall without thinking onto the kneeler.

My compact rental is dwarfed by pickups as I cross the Mississippi at Baton Rouge and enter the Atchafalaya Basin, a landscape of tupelo and cypress swamps. The water tower in Breaux Bridge proclaims the small city the *Crawfish Capital of the World*. I exit the interstate at Lafayette and head south. Magnolias flaunt flowers the size of dinner plates. Dollar Generals and tackle shops punctuate take-out shacks advertising *boudin* and *cracklins*. A two-and-a-half-hour drive west of New Orleans, this is the heart of Cajun Country. Bayou Teche cuts through the landscape with a series of towns along its banks. I slow down as I approach St. Martin Parish, known for its quaint downtown, sugarcane production, crawfish, hot sauce, and now a priest who drives a mobile confessional. The closer I get to Father Champagne, the larger the confessional looms. I begin to make more stops than necessary, getting water and gas and pulling over to look at bayous, egrets, and live oaks.

In St. Martinville Father Champagne shows me around the Community of Jesus Christ Crucified, pointing out the retreat center, the sisters' housing, the chapel, and a newly acquired building used as a food pantry and tutoring center. Drawing on Father Champagne's creative leadership, the small community of contemplative missionaries hosts an eighty-eight-hour marathon reading of the Bible in the town square and organizes the annual *Fete-Dieu du Teche*, a fifty-boat eucharistic procession down Bayou Teche every August on the Feast of the Assumption. After Vespers the black-cassocked Father Champagne invites me to stay for a planning meeting for *Fete-Dieu du Teche*. As I follow him through the courtyard, I'm struck by the fragrance of flowers.

"Confederate jasmine," Father Champagne says. I bend into the blooming vine; its perfume startles me as much as the sight of evening primrose clustered along swampy roadsides had the day before. I'd stopped to take photos of the delicate pink bells at a pull-off where other travelers had stood looking for gators. A wonder, I thought, how such tenderness survives.

Father Champagne invites me to ride along in the Spiritual Care Unit the next day. The first stop is ten miles south, in New Iberia. We pass over railroad tracks and under live oaks, drive by fading cottages, grand old houses, and businesses named for the Acadian folk hero Evangeline – Evangeline Funeral Home, Evangeline Optical, Evangeline Coca-Cola Bottling. Cajuns are fiercely proud of their heritage, which includes Catholicism and is part of the reason for their ancestors' expulsion from Canada two hundred fifty years ago.

We pull into Lagniappe Village and park outside a Subway shop. They have the routine down. The sisters pull out portable steps, unfold a table, and load it with materials – including an Examination of Conscience brochure listing the Works of Mercy and Seven Deadly Sins. A portable loudspeaker plays French hymns.

We park for two hours, as people drive in and out of the strip mall to buy pet food, get their nails done, or pick up a foot-long for lunch. Most smile and wave. Many come over, hug the sisters, and thank them for their work. They ask for prayers, offer to buy lunch, or stand waiting their turn for confession. A few shoppers ignore the confessional, which – with the music and life-sized image of Jesus fixed to its side – is tough to do.

The sisters had talked about their most enthusiastic supporter before she arrived – I'll call her Evangeline in deference to the region, but also because of her unswerving bent toward evangelization. "If Miss Evangeline were here, she'd get them to come to confession," the sisters said when a trio of workers emerged from a car and failed to look our way.

They had not exaggerated. When she arrives, Evangeline flits around the parking lot, all blonde hair and *hey y'alls*. She uses her boundless enthusiasm to coax people into the confessional, and, just as the sun breaks loose from the clouds during a slow spell, settles her gaze on me.

"You going in?"

"I'm not sure." I try to sound casual, as if Miss Evangeline's offering sweet tea.

"You're Catholic, aren't you?"

I wipe the sweat from my brow and nod, wondering if she can sense just how recently I've returned and how tenuous it all seems as I stand beside the ambulance with the light fixed to the top – green to indicate it's free, red to show that Father Champagne's sitting with someone. Right now the light is green, and Evangeline sees that I see.

"Have you gone to confession lately?" Her voice is two parts cotton candy, one part fishing knife.

"Yes," I say, adding lying to the list of sins I may never confess. "But I'm just observing today."

"What better way to observe than from inside," Evangeline says and, even as my heart starts flailing around in my chest, I have to admit that she's right.

Southern Louisiana is not for the faint of heart. Catfish grow larger than dogs. Schools close on the first Friday in October for squirrel-hunting day. There's no vegetarian patty at the New Iberia Subway, and to ask for one is like driving a Prius with a Hillary bumper sticker into a land of Ford F-150s decked out with antler decals and hunting racks. When Miss Evangeline reports that she has 1,200 frog legs in her freezer, I don't for a second doubt it and try my best to wipe sympathy for all six hundred frogs from my face.

Which is to say that I am faint of heart.

I'm afraid of house centipedes, of baiting a hook, of the suspect texture of ill-cooked okra, of the proliferation of germs, of navigating bendy roadways, and of looking down from great heights. And despite the fact that I've traveled a thousand miles to learn about his project and have within me struggles and conflicts and a desire to confess – despite all this, in this moment of baking under the sun in rural Louisiana, more than anything, I'm afraid to step inside the Spiritual Care Unit, sit across from Father Champagne, and let loose with all my sins.

Before heading to St. Martinville I'd met a friend for breakfast in New Orleans. I told him where I was going, explaining the mobile confessional, my interest in the sacrament, and the fact that it seems in danger of falling away.

"Really?" He leaned in. "I always thought confession would be the best part of being Catholic."

"How so?" I bit into the deep-fried potato salad I'd ordered with scrambled eggs. Seasoned with a touch of mustard, the side dish was delectable and five kinds of sin itself.

"You know, just sitting there and getting to talk," he said. "Like therapy."

"But it's not therapy," I shook my head. "It's not an airing of grievances or a list of various hurts. It's the owning of faults and bad choices. It's saying to another human being, *Here's what I did wrong.*"

"Oh," he said. "Never mind."

But even as we laughed, the image of confessing to a priest flashed before me, so real and so frightening I considered another order of fried potato salad to hold it at bay.

If it were merely a matter of revelation, I'd have hopped into the Spiritual Care Unit before Miss Evangeline ever arrived on the scene. It's not confession I struggle with so much as contrition. I'm not alone in this. Perhaps in reaction to once being so bound, the culture has largely thrown off shame and made revelation a pastime. Round-the-clock access to the electronic signals of others facilitates our sharing. Maybe we haven't abandoned confession so much as traded in one screen for another.

Guilt is a useless emotion, an old boyfriend once said. We were the *Free-to-Be* generation, attenders of Buddhist weekends and readers of Herman Hesse, Joseph Campbell, *Our Bodies, Ourselves*. What earlier generations called sin we reframed as personality quirks or, if especially troublesome, the result of the particular constellations of our childhoods. This was liberating in many ways and preferable to the binds we saw in the older generation who seemed as committed to their chronic sense of obligation as we were to its eradication. But hadn't we become flip sides of the same coin – as dwarfed by our commitment to bliss as our parents had been by denying theirs? So that, along with the rise of the public confessional, our sense of responsibility has dramatically withered and, for better or worse, we've entered the post-contrition era.

This is compounded by shifting notions of sin. Many of the sins espoused by the Church are simply no longer accepted as sinful by society, including many Catholics. Birth control. Divorce. Same-sex love. The divide between institutionally sanctioned morality and the way people live has grown exponentially over the past few decades. Clerical abuses and the resulting scandals have only intensified the rift. More and more Catholics have chosen to stay home – if not from church, then certainly from the confessional.

Which brings me back to Louisiana, where the only booth I slip into is inside the Subway restaurant as the community eats after finishing confessions. I slump and avoid Evangeline's eye as I nibble a spinach and cucumber sandwich.

They'd been so generous. Why had I failed to partake? Was it because I'm in a conservative part of the country and fear my sense of sin would contrast glaringly with their own? Partly. But it's more than that.

When I asked Father Champagne earlier in the day why he thought confession was falling away, he said even Catholics have become doggedly individualistic and American in our approach to everything, including God.

"Our temptation is toward isolation," he said. "We think we can do it all ourselves."

"We don't want to be vulnerable before another human being," I said, and if I'd used an "I" in place of "we," I might have begun my own confession right there.

I update my Facebook and Instagram pages a few times a week and have written about myself in essays and poems – but it's somehow easier to bare my soul to unseen thousands than to open myself to one human being sitting quietly before me. As I've once again made myself at home in the pew, I'm discovering that the sacraments confer grace in direct proportion to our willingness to open ourselves to them, and if we are, in fact, one body – despite the way we so often sequester ourselves in the whir of our own activity – then this opening of the self to another is nothing less than sacred.

My friend Mary says confession is like getting a carwash for your soul. *You feel so good after, all clean and bright.* If she were in St. Martinville, she'd have tossed aside her walker, jumped into the Spiritual Care Unit, and outdone even Evangeline at getting others to follow suit. I love Mary like nobody's business, but I'm a gifted excuse-maker, and even if she could have been whisked from her nursing home in Rochester to the Spiritual Care Unit in New Iberia decked out with her throng of saints' medals and Padre Pio cross, I'd have found a way to stay planted in the parking lot.

No, I did not confess in the Spiritual Care Unit that day. But I sat two feet from the kneeler on the return to St. Martinville and read an Act of Contrition on the back of a prayer card and talked quietly with the novice. "Have you ever been in an ambulance?" she asked, and it took me a minute to realize I had not. How lucky I've been, I thought as we passed again under live oaks. It was this, perhaps, and Father Champagne's example, the startling scent of jasmine – even the proselytizing Miss Evangeline with all those frog legs in her freezer – that propelled me home and into a seat across from my parish priest. And no matter what I said – the various failings and delusions and roadblocks I admitted to, no matter how awkward the chug of my words or how makeshift my Act of Contrition – he sat there, anointing by listening, blessing with hands and words and goodness itself, before sending me back out into the broken, beautiful world to begin again.

11

In Persona Christi

The girl beside me is beautiful but does not know it. This is not unusual. The room is filled with people who do not see their own beauty.

"Happy Thanksgiving," the priest says as the men file in. Father Bob arrived after celebrating an earlier Mass and sounded so hoarse I did not think he'd manage another. Now he's all movement and reaching out – greeting people, lining up first and second readers. His cold is bad enough that he'll miss Thanksgiving with family and friends but he did not cancel this service. No matter how sick, there's clearly nowhere he'd rather be. Watching him now is like watching a small but spectacular fireworks display. Even his gray hair is slightly frizzed, as if the energy pulsing through his body has had its way.

"Did you have anything special to eat today?" Father Bob is asking. I'd already asked this of the young woman seated next to me but listen as others list items from their holiday meal.

"Turkey," someone calls out.

"Cranberry sauce."

"Milk," a few say.

"Apple cake," my girl adds, then whispers, "But that was some mushy shit."

We sit in chairs the color of gumdrops. Mass is held in a classroom today because the holiday has shifted the schedule, making the gymnasium unavailable. Walls are peppered with motivational slogans. Posters championing positive thinking are tacked beside charts presenting random math concepts (mean vs. median vs. mode) and signs highlighting the basic components of grammar (prepositions, interjections, adverbs).

I calculate the median age of the room to be about twenty-five and note that the girl on my right has an excellent grasp of interjection. Despite the actual range of ages, everyone seems young. This is because of the holiday, perhaps, or the bright posters and molded plastic chairs. Either way, I'm struck by the thought that we're a bunch of children cast in different roles: the inmates in their jumpsuits; the deputies with guns at their hips and loops of jangly keys; the priest who has draped a stole embroidered with autumn colors over his long white robe; and me, staring wide-eyed and trying to take it all in – the educational posters, the deputy seated with a crossword puzzle at a desk, the priest making the sign of the cross to begin.

The men arrived first. Twelve or so. After they were seated, the women were led through the back door and sat behind them. The men must not turn around. This is the rule. When I was introduced I walked from the women's section to the front to say hello so they would not twist in their chairs and see the female inmates. They could not see, for instance, the long blond braid of the woman who read the psalm. One man's head turned instinctively toward the sound of her voice but he caught himself and missed the way she furrowed her brow as she tried her best to pronounce such fine and faraway words.

It's always this way. Men in front, women in back, deputies watching from desks and doorframes. My niece explained this when I visited her last year, along with a rundown of jumpsuit colors and what they mean. *We don't go up front for Communion,* she said. *Someone walks back to our section.*

I came to the jail to observe Mass because I've been trying to work out for some time what makes Father Bob special. To someone who's never had a father – kindly or otherwise – the possibility of a good one offers an irresistible pull. I scan the room and imagine that, in this, I'm probably not alone. But this doesn't fully explain my fascination with my parish priest. Instead, I have a sense that he has something to teach me. The trick is to figure out what it might be. Whatever it is, I suspect, happens here. But as I look around, I wonder whether I've also come to see what my niece has seen during the times she's been locked inside this very same space.

And now, bless the God of all,
Who has done wondrous things on earth . . .

The man reading from the scriptures is one of the youngest in the room. Even with his back turned, everything about him is fine. A few of the women lean in as he reads, imagining perhaps the well-formed mouth. They watch as he tucks a thicket of dark waves behind an ear. *The Word of the Lord,* he says at the end, and his voice is so earnest that the girl next to me flops her head into her lap and nearly comes undone inside a cathedral of laughter and hair.

Earlier I'd helped dress the altar. It was only a long folding table until the cloth was added and a cross.

"This is our credence table," Father Bob proclaimed, and more than setting the cruet and paten onto the hospital-style side table, the sheer conviction of his proclamation transformed it into sacred space.

Supplies came from a footlocker, padlocked with the word CATHOLIC written in capital letters across the top. As we unloaded it, I imagined other lockers stored in a utility closet somewhere in the belly of the jail – a series of black trunks marked ISLAMIC, JEWISH, PROTESTANT. And though I later noticed that my end of the altar cloth hung unevenly and the cross I'd placed was not precisely centered, I understood that helping to arrange the altar was the best thing I'd do all day.

Later I will eat stuffing and squash and four kinds of pie. Later my mother-in-law will make a game of questions to remind us of the real history of the Pilgrims and the Wampanoag. Later there will be nieces and nephews pointed straight as arrows toward Brown, Cornell, and Princeton. And not just in-laws – a few of my own relations are headed toward the kind of success we can all agree upon. The day after Thanksgiving I'll walk with my sister's family around a pond strung with grasses lit by afternoon sun. Later still I'll talk with my sister about church and her silence will flood my ears.

"Don't most educated people eventually drop religion?" she finally says when I don't drop the subject. "And object to all the bad done in its name?"

"Of course," I say to the last half of the question and press on. When did I become so adamant? I don't like to argue with this sister, mostly because she usually wins but also because our fears are more aligned than she realizes, and I won't be adequate to the believer's role into which I've somehow cast myself.

"We worry about the mingling of church and state," she says and describes a newsletter her husband subscribes to on that very issue.

"I worry about that too," I say but get the sense she doesn't believe, that there's either church or no church, and I'm kidding myself to consider anything in between. Maybe I am. Still, it's always bothered me, the way we box ourselves in with labels and words. Some of the most loving people I know don't consider themselves religious. Some of the most embittered do. We know the futility of such distinctions on some level and still how stuck we are.

I think of the grammar poster at the jail and how the most important parts of speech are often those left unsaid. I think of our brother's death this past spring and how this very same sister wanted a priest and church service. I think of the food baskets and donations that got us through the holidays when we were kids, the refrigerator the church once gave our mother when we had none, our years in and out of parochial schools, and the Sisters of St. Joseph teaching flocks of city kids for a pittance and little thanks.

But as much as I consider its tradition of charity and social justice, our church was more to us than handouts, and the loss of neighborhood churches is more than the loss of food pantries and homeless shelters. I want to tell my sister how the Mass somehow unclenches my heart, but fear such talk will mark me as far gone. Ah, but now I've strayed into the land mines of family and religion when what I most want to share is the round of giggles that erupts when Father Bob says *open your missals* and the girl beside me hears *missiles*.

"Now, I know this group can sing." Father Bob's accent is pure western New York – flattened vowels joined to the more fluid inflections imparted to the cities by generations of European immigrants. His voice is marked by the patina of familiarity common to regulars at diners or neighborhood bars, but is inlaid with the sort of dramatic pauses and emphatic declaratives that would do a Southern preacher proud. He harnesses all of this to encourage those assembled to sing the *Alleluia* – making a production of every syllable while raising his brows in a dramatic show of admiration. "You sound awesome," he says. "You could be performing as a choir down on Main Street."

Everyone laughs, both nervous and relieved, because singing can be so much harder than talking. Most at least try. The priest points out the liturgical responses as he goes, breaks the prayers into sections, helps a young man serve at the altar by showing him how to extend the vessel of water and when to offer the towel.

An older woman who knows the words to every prayer trumpets them from her seat and leads the women's section with the backbeat of her voice. When the time comes, she offers an intention for her family. "Especially for my daughter, Ruby," she says.

"Oh my goodness," the girl beside me gushes. "That is such a pretty name."

If I were as gifted at interjection as she is, I'd cut in and say that she too is a gem. Instead, I stay quiet until the time for the *Our Father* comes and we stand. It's normal at church to hold hands at this juncture, but I'm not sure what to expect here. The girl senses my hesitation and waits a beat before taking mine. The warmth of her hand surprises me. Mine is cold. "Don't worry," she says when I apologize. She doesn't know all the words to the prayer, but recites the few she's memorized. *Give us this day*, she says. *Our daily bread*.

If the classroom had a poster of ecclesiastical Latin, *in persona Christi* might appear in italic letters, along with *caritas, veritas,* and *sanctus, sanctus, sanctus*.

In persona Christi refers to actions of the priest in his role as a stand-in for Jesus. A priest is believed to be acting in the person of Christ when he confers the sacraments, for instance, which is why we entrust him with the breaking of bread, anointing of bodies, and hearing of confessions. While central to the priest's role, a muddled version of the same concept might explain the culture of clericalism and sexism, and how abuses were tolerated for so long. That such manipulation was handed down in God's name accounts for the betrayal that runs so deep and why many recoil from the Church's centuries-long hold.

But human beings are also capable of profound goodness. Didn't the actual person of Christ turn the world on its head with that premise two thousand years ago? That some clerics do not act *in persona Christi* is unquestionable. As is the fact that clerics and laypeople alike are called to do so, and the parsing and consignment of such holy orders to a clerical class has limited our growth while forcing unrealistic expectations on the few who take them on. How can we be shocked when such a setup fails? But here's the miracle: sometimes it goes right, and when it does there's nothing like it in the world.

"Advent is just around the corner." Now Father Bob's wrapping up Mass and preparing his small flock for next week and the change of the liturgical season.

We turn our faces to him like flowers following the sun. This is not too grand a comparison because a certain jubilant energy spreads out in his wake.

"Christmas isn't something you click on and off like a string of lights," he's saying as the deputies begin to shift their weight and jingle keys at the door. "You can't have a good Christmas without a good Advent."

Earlier he'd talked about gratitude, and a woman who comes to help with the Mass shared a quote she'd read from Saint Thérèse of Lisieux about gratitude attracting God.

"Interesting." The priest had rubbed the divot of his lip with a slender finger like a professor considering an intriguing idea. "We already know we're loved by God a hundred percent no matter what," he'd said. "But being grateful helps attract him to us – how about that?"

The men and women heard the message – *You are loved* – but did not lean in until he began his Advent talk. Calendars are important here. Looking forward is something this particular congregation understands. Making ready. Waiting expectantly. Counting down days.

"That cough doesn't sound any better," I say when I call a few days later to ask about altar servers and how they're recruited at the correctional facility. The priest had submitted to a bout of intense coughing once the Mass had ended, racking him so hard I wished for the first time we were not in jail but in an ordinary place with a vat of hot water and tea. "Some have been altar boys in the past," he's saying, "but mostly it's on-the-job training."

"And actually," he adds, "I'm getting better every day."

"Good," I say but am not convinced. He could be dying and make the same claim.

"I'm taking a Puerto Rican remedy," he explains. The parish is home to a large Puerto Rican community and someone has clearly hooked our beloved priest up with a cure. A mixture of aloe, honey and lime. When I ask if he drinks it warm, he says no.

"You need to heat it up," I say. "And add some whiskey."

He laughs a bit while I wonder what provokes me to say such idiotic things – though in truth the whiskey would help, as would the heat, and the greater truth is that, like the parishioners plying him with cures, I need Father Bob to be well. Because he's a good priest, yes. Because he anoints the dying and buries the homeless and shows up every day for those who need him. Because he celebrates daily Masses, nursing home Masses, Catholic Worker and Pax Christi Masses, *quinceañera* Masses, school Masses, *Nuestra Señora* and holy day Masses, wedding Masses and funeral Masses and Sunday Masses every weekend times three – and, at seventy-three, has even taught himself to preach some of those homilies in Spanish. Because he hears confessions, baptizes babies, organizes neighborhood festivals and antidrug walks. Because he serves on committees for Martin Luther King Day, antipoverty initiatives, and neighborhood renewal. Because he stands with black Catholics and female Catholics and any-other-person-Catholic-or-non-Catholic, all while shepherding three distinct city communities clustered into one parish.

All of this, yes.

But if Father Bob's magic is primarily one of sacrifice, why have I been so slow to figure it out and why am I so cautious now to extol its virtues? Perhaps I fear it will ring false to praise his dedication without recognizing that his burden is so great precisely because it's left to so few. And I say with no disrespect for the bottomlessness of his devotion and the sanctity of his tasks that his genius lies less in their management than in the way he looks into each face and says, *Thanks be to God.*

This is why I need our priest to be well.

Because no matter how much I'd like to believe otherwise, I'm not simply watching and writing words on a page. I need him to drink potions of aloe and whiskey and whatever else it takes because I recognized the girl at the jail as my sister, my niece, myself. Because I saw the man turning toward the sound of a sweet voice as my brother, my nephew, my very same self.

It seems to me that we're all in that room waiting to be seen. That's why he matters so much. Our astonishing extravagant wholly human saint of a priest. Because sometimes, while seated in a gumdrop-colored chair, a woman will catch sight of her own beauty in the good Father's eyes. And it will be enough – just enough – to help her lift her voice in song, to bend whatever words she knows into prayer, and to summon the exquisite courage needed to reach out and take another's hand.

SEARCH FOR THE VIRGIN, PART VI

Buffalo

The Buffalo Religious Arts Center is loaded with Marys. She appears on icons, tapestries, and stained glass – and even in the name of its founder, Mary Holland.

I'm done looking for the Virgin, I'd said to myself while breathing in the clean scent of pine in the light-filled space of Buffalo's cathedral. It felt right as I said it and I thought about how much the journey had meant, no matter the outcome, as I headed east along the thruway.

A newfound wisdom had descended, it seemed. An enlightened capitulation and profound letting go. It was deep and mature and lasted about an hour.

Back in Rochester, I opened an email from a Buffalo church. It described a local Religious Arts Center, which houses artifacts from closed churches, and advised me to check there. "I'm all about Our Lady," wrote Rosemary from Assumption Church. "I hope you find her!"

I immediately reached out to the Arts Center and its founder to find out more. After reading of the impending closures of seventy Buffalo churches in 2007, Mary Holland began to visit them, admiring the architecture and unique fixtures while wondering what would become of the buildings and the treasures they housed. Not content to simply wonder, she bought St. Francis Xavier in the Black Rock neighborhood and transformed the old

German church into a space to preserve and showcase sacred objects from closed worship sites in western New York.

She's collected stained glass and statues, but also saved blueprints, old photographs, and prayer books in the many languages once spoken in Black Rock. Each object tells the story of people who sacrificed everything to build the grandest buildings they could. Sacred spaces in which to celebrate, give thanks, and pray for better days. And when those places folded – when their children and grandchildren left and the buildings were wrecked or repurposed or sold – the paintings and statues and candlesticks required another sanctuary. In Buffalo, thanks to Mary Holland, they have one.

This was a woman who would understand my quest.

"I want to see what you've done," I say when I call to arrange a visit. "But my Mary is from Rochester and I don't expect to find her there."

"I have some pieces from Rochester," she says. "From Corpus Christi Church."

"Corpus Christi?" The thump of blood is so loud in my ears, I can't be certain I've heard. Buffalo has a Corpus Christi parish, which I'd visited only last week. "In Rochester?"

"An Our Lady of Lourdes." She goes on to describe a corresponding Bernadette with an unusual plaid jacket. "I've never seen one like it."

"Mine is an Our Lady of Grace model," I interrupt. "With a blue cloak."

"Yes," she says, as if the statue sounds familiar, but describes a crowned Virgin standing on a globe.

"Oh." My heart falls back into its socket. "My Mary has no crown."

I recall the glut of statues from my first Christmas Eve back at church a few years ago and realize that the Buffalo Religious Arts Center could house a boatload of Rochester Marys and still not have mine. But there's a chance. I want to hop on the thruway and drive the sixty miles to Buffalo this minute, but the region's been pummeled by Christmas storms with some roads still impassable.

We settle on the end of the week and I begin to flare with bouts of hope and despair. I call my old friend Mary to update her on the hunt, but she can listen for only so long before blurting out a solution so obvious, she can no longer hold it in.

"If you want to find that statue, honey, you better ask Saint Anthony for help."

I laugh but she does not. To Mary, Saint Anthony is to lost objects what aspirin is to headaches. And despite my clumsiness with prayer, later that day I go to the bookcase and find the tiny retablo I brought back from Albuquerque. I hold the painted rectangle of wood in my hand, marveling at the gentleness of the saint's expression. On the reverse side is written: *San Antonio de Padua. 1195–1231. Finder of lost objects and worthy husbands.* I close my eyes and try to think of what to say while blotting out the image of Mary tssking me for not turning to the saint back when my search first began.

"Okay, Saint Anthony." I look out the window at the snow still coming down. "This is my last shot. Please let my Mary be there."

12

Holy Water

When I arrive at the well, the gate does not give.

As I head back to the car, another couple pull in and emerge from their seats with a bucket and trowels. They're here to tend a grave – or several graves, more probably – and may know as many people under the ground as are seated in Considine's pub across the way.

"When does the well open?" The cottage we've rented is an hour up the coast, and though my husband is interested in the nearby cliffs as a lookout for puffins, I can't be certain we'll pass this way again.

"Oh, it never closes." The man leads me back to the gate, reaches over and unclicks the latch. He must help a hundred tourists a year but does so with good cheer.

"There you are," he says.

St. Brigid's Well lies on a much-traveled road south of the Cliffs of Moher. We'd pulled away from the admission booths and visitor center at the Cliffs, driven past O'Brien's Tower and the Hag's Head – until Liscannor Bay came into view. We'd gorged on beauty after only a few days of Irish coastline. The views of the sea and stretches of green fields with roses spilling onto stone walls had repeated themselves so often a sluggishness had set in and we let them pass without mention.

"Just in there now." The man motions past a life-sized statue of Saint Brigid toward a whitewashed building set against the hill. This is the *Ula íochtarach* or lower sanctuary. The tunnel-

like grotto is open at the rear, offering a view of water trickling
in through layers of stone and the boughs of an overhead tree
tied with strips of bright cloth. A *clootie tree*, it's called, and,
like holy wells, such trees can be found in Celtic sites throughout the British Isles. But I only learn this after the fact. I know
nothing as the man nods a final time before turning back and
I step into the grotto.

The body is more water than anything else. We learned this in
grade school, along with the names of oceans and seas and major
rivers of the world. We were given maps of the continents and
maps of the body and used the same blue crayon to color the
Atlantic Ocean as the cytoplasm in a human cell. If our teachers were especially committed, they listed the percentages of
water in our major organs:

> *Heart and brain* – 73%
> *Lungs* – 83%
> *Muscles and kidneys* – 79%
> *Skin* – 65%
> *Bones* – 32%

Even the bones! we cried, thinking of Halloween skeletons
and the dryness of cookies without milk. *Yes,* they nodded.
Even the bones. Water insulates, they said. It helps to regu-
late temperature, to metabolize food, and to flush waste. It
lubricates the joints, protects the organs, and provides safe
harbor for our offspring. It's the building block of each of our
trillions of cells.

Water is holy. Our teachers did not say this. They would not
sully their science lessons with such a word. But neither could
they restrain their reverence for a substance with a greater hold
on us than our own mothers.

When a Catholic enters a church, she dips her fingers into a
font near the entrance and crosses herself. This is a holdover

from the days when people walked through dusty lands to get to church. Stones caught in their sandals. The sun flared. Cypress trees offered only needles of shade. The faithful arrived sweat-streaked and cleaned themselves in basins or simple fountains placed near entrances for that purpose. Centuries later the Catholic performs a vestige of this act. She gathers water with the tips of her fingers. It's nearly magnetic, the way the droplets cling to her flesh. She brings her fingers to her forehead, her breastbone, and along the collarbone at left and right shoulder to make the sign upon her body.

She does not think as she does this. Water is closer than thought. She was sealed in its chamber as she tumbled forth in the spring of her mother's womb – back when her arms and legs were only buds and the slits in her flesh looked like gills. Back before she was a woman or girl and more like a tiny fish.

It's a reservoir of desire, the well dedicated to Saint Brigid at Liscannor.

Mementos plaster the walls, dangle from rafters, and overflow from every last crevice. Photographs and prayer cards. Crosses and medals. Obituaries and assorted personal objects: a spoon tucked into a tangle of rosaries; a pink teacup set into a baby doll's lap; a blue ribbon marked *2nd Place, Equestrian*; laces from a child's shoe.

A wide ledge running the length of the grotto swells with statues. Many are missing hands or elbows or toes. Moisture has penetrated their painted cloaks, causing them to rupture and crumble. They stand side by side and lean into each other for support, an army of beleaguered saints. Jesus is plentiful: there are several Sacred Hearts, a Crucified Christ, two Infants of Prague. Saint Theresa and Padre Pio are well represented. A tulip-shaped flame erupts from Jude's head. A bird perches on Francis's shoulder. Joseph holds the sleeping Child. But no figure is as ubiquitous as the Blessed Mother. The Virgins range in height from a few inches to a foot and are crafted of plaster and ceramic and glass. A Japanese Madonna joins Our Lady of Mt. Carmel and a Virgin with Eastern eyes and an old-world crown. The statues are strung with so many rosaries they nearly disappear under the swath of beads.

My eye lands on a delicate-faced Mary. Moss blooms on her mantle, rendering it the color of river water. Behind her, a framed portrait of Saint Anthony with the Infant. A print of the Immaculate Heart overlaps an image of Our Lady of Perpetual Help. Snapshots are tucked into the frames: a child crawling on a carpeted floor in some faraway house; an ultrasound image, grainy and dark; a woman from the 1950s, skirt flaring from a fitted waist, hand on hip, striking a saucy pose. They are the sort of framed pieces that once hung on grandmothers' living room walls – perhaps more than anything, the grotto is a thousand grandmothers' walls.

The water glints with coins. Sunlight filters through the tree overhead. A tendril of ivy pushes through a crack and grows along the wall. I turn and stare, sensing that something is required of me, but what?

Unsure of what to do, I kneel before the water, wet my fingers and cross myself, as if the well were a stoup and the whole of Ireland a church.

Though the well is devoted to Brigid, water probably flowed from Liscannor before the fifth century, when the saint is said to have been born to an enslaved woman named Brocca. The girl did not have a father so much as a master by whom she and her mother were owned. Brigid was marked early by God. She was suckled by a white cow, they say. She could stop the wind and rain, multiply portions of milk and butter, and heal others – including a leper whose disease was washed away by a cup of blessed water. In this way Saint Brigid bore striking similarities to the ancient Celtic goddess of the same name. Born at the exact moment of daybreak, the goddess Brigid was said to keep an enchanted orchard from which her bees carried magical honey. Shamrocks appeared wherever she stepped. Who can say for certain when the time of the goddess began, but there would have been water before then – back when people had no language for what they found and marked the wells with a pile of rocks, the petals of a gentian, the bones of a hare tied to the branches of a hawthorn tree.

Water gurgled as Patrick tramped through Ireland. It flowed as monasteries were built and manuscripts copied and illuminated. It sprang when the Vikings came to plunder, when Henry II set the first royal English foot onto Irish soil, and, centuries later, when Cromwell followed suit. The wells kept running as land was confiscated, churches were leveled, and people took to them to ask for blessings on what remained. They came to the Liscannor well from the Aran Islands and all over County Clare, chanting prayers and using candles to light their paths.

Even the Protestant landlord partook. When he fell sick in England in 1840, Cornelius O'Brien was said to send for water from the well and credited it with his cure. O'Brien is famous for the observation tower he built at the nearby cliffs but is also believed to have restored the well – providing stone housing, grooming the pathways, and surrounding the sanctuary with an iron fence. Odd perhaps, an Irish Protestant solidifying a site associated with Roman Catholic ritual, but the well belongs to everyone. *It never closes*, the man had said as he let me in, meaning the well-house and the sanctuary, but he might as well have meant the water itself, which came long before and will continue on after all of us.

I was brought to the font on a sunny day in autumn. Locust trees and sugar maples flamed on the streets surrounding Corpus Christi as inside the ingredients for baptism were assembled: infant and priest; oil and holy water. Only a father was missing. There was no man at my mother's elbow, no one to slip a twenty into Father McCabe's hand after Mass. Metaphorical fathers abounded – the kindly priest, the molded gospel writers perched along the high altar, even God in heaven – but these were symbols and statues and theological constructs, none of whom would show in the snapshots.

My mother had separated from her husband years before, but that did not stop her from continuing to present infants for baptism, each arriving with an entirely different set of features. Baptism, the Church proclaimed, replaced original sin with the grace of God. But to my mother the ritual was less about sin than the confluence of water, stained glass, and light. If she was ashamed, she did not show it. She came to Mass with her parade of mismatched children and, on a clear Sunday in October, swaddled me in white and watched as the priest invoked the Trinity and poured water three times over my head.

Even if I'd had a father or siblings whose faces matched my own, the priest would have spoken the same blessing – *in the name of the Father, and of the Son, and of the Holy Spirit* – as water ran from my forehead onto my dress and into the reddish tufts of hair. Water, like sacrament itself, does not change according to who receives it. I might have been a Vanderbilt, a Kennedy, or the child of the goddess Brigid herself – wrapped in raw silk and crowned by honeybees – and the water would have trickled from my head onto the floor tiles in precisely the same way.

It's the nature of water to rise and fall. It evaporates from oceans and puddles and fattens the clouds until it returns to earth as snow or rain and runs into rivers and streams and swamps. It's taken up by the loosestrife growing in the creek and by the fox as he licks the edge of the pond. It's taken up by buckets and a network of underground pipes. It's chugged and sweat and spat. It's filtered by soil and metal tubing and chemical wash. It does not stay put. Rivers meander and break into lakes. Mountaintop streams feed muddy creeks that slog into rivers and head again to the sea, so that the water the fox sips and the loosestrife takes up is the same Patrick used to baptize the slave Brocca; the same Brocca used to wipe the face of her newborn; the same Brigid filtered through chamomile and nettle to make tea for her sister nuns; the same that swirled inside my mother as the man rose from her bed and she turned on her pillow and slept.

On Pentecost the priest sprinkles the congregation with water. Aspersion, it's called, and the tool in his hands an aspergillum. He does the same to bless the palms on Palm Sunday, on Easter, at funeral Masses, at house blessings, and sometimes, it seems to me, when he's in a certain celebratory mood. He circles the church, launching droplets onto shoulders and faces and hair.

It's an ancient practice, the sprinkling of water to purify. Leviticus describes binding a living bird with string dyed from an insect found on the leaves of certain Mediterranean oaks – insects so round and red they were originally thought to be berries. The scarlet thread bound the bird to a cedar plank, which worked as a handle to scatter liquid from a broom of tail feathers and hyssop, after which the bird was freed.

Modern clerics rely on aspergilla fashioned of metal with long handles and reservoirs of holy water at one end. A priest no longer uses red thread or hyssop – though the water may as well be sifted through a broom of feathers and blooming mint for how cool it feels as it lands on the face.

When I ask my husband to return to the well on our last day in County Clare, I only know that I want to return and little else. I don't know, for instance, to bend deep at the knee and look for the trout said to dwell deep inside the well. I don't know to collect water in plastic bottles shaped like the Blessed Mother, nor do I know to remove my shoes and circle the sanctuary barefoot while offering prayers to Brigid the goddess and Brigid the saint and Brocca whose body was the first well Brigid ever knew.

Instead, I write the names of those I love on a postcard featuring the wild flowers of Ireland and leave it against a flaking statue of Martin de Porres.

Just a few days between visits, but already the grotto has shifted. In a month how different it will look. In a year another batch of mementos will arise, old names will give way to new: Linda O'Brien from Tipperary and the McDermotts, William and Mary, wiped from sight. Snapshots will be taped over and lost: the beauty smiling in her wedding dress, the crew of workers in plaid shirts clinking coffee mugs, the toddler perched and pouting on the back of a Mercedes. Letters will fade until messages can no longer be read:

RIP John McGowan.

I love you, Daddy.

To Saint Brigid, Please make Kay Weatheral better to get rid of her cancer.

It's an ever-blooming and collective collage of loss, the holy well. But, this time, at least, I know why I've come. I'm here for the sight of silk dahlias and plaster Jesuses and a child's stuffed whale wilting side by side. I'm here for the echo of water and the loamy scent of earth. Such things are as breathtaking to me as the flock of puffins nesting in the hummocky turf on nearby cliffs.

To make water holy, a priest speaks prayers over it. To chase the devil away, some add a pinch of salt. It delights me to imagine my parish priest pouring his breath over water, the weight of the task furrowing his brow. But as much as I've grown used to the reverberation of his voice in the building on East Main Street – something more elemental unfolds from the well. Moisture fixes itself to my hair as I think of mothers and fathers and sacraments more ancient than the Church. It's a reminder, the holy well. Of the unrelenting press of human longing, yes, and the ferocity of our thirst, but of something else besides. A scarlet thread binding the fifth century to 1840 to 1968; a spray of feathers linking Brocca to O'Brien to my mother; a hundred thousand forgotten names settling like droplets onto the skin.

I turn to leave but stop for one last look at the flood of hard things (statues and teacups and rosary beads) going soft in the grotto – everything greening – even as it fades.

13

The Marigold Parade

The grocery store is swamped with roses tonight. Thousands of long-stems. Pink and yellow miniatures in ceramic pots. Bouquets with lilies and baby's breath. Petals by the bagful. It's as if a flower market has erupted in the space the zucchini and clementines normally occupy. People buzz around the display like oversized bees, the population in that section of the store alone outranks the number of people at church.

Ash Wednesday and Valentine's Day have landed on the same date this year. *From dust you came and to dust you shall return* coupled with chocolate and red foil hearts. Last year I'd gone to Sacred Heart for ashes. Just over the river in Richmond, in a neighborhood of old warehouses and a Central American congregation, the bilingual service had reminded me of my Rochester church. This year, instead of being reminded of home, I'm actually home. I want to say this is wonderful, except that I'm one of three English speakers at Mass, and, on this day, which is also Valentine's Day, I feel strangely alone in the pew. There's the sense that the bilingual service – in which entire sections of the liturgy are repeated – is largely unnecessary. Were it not for the other two English speakers, I'd go to the priest and say *no need to do the English on my behalf, Father.* Instead, I listen to the homily in Spanish, then English, stand in line for ashes, and skip out to the grocery store for bananas and sparkling water.

In truth I'm hoping for more than bananas and water. I'd like to find a heart-shaped box of chocolates – the old-fashioned variety with velvet bows and lace trim. Because it's late in the day, and the holiday has nearly passed, I'd also like the heart to be half-price. I won't eat the candy on this, the first day of Lent. Instead, I'll store my discount heart in the trunk of my car and feel better knowing it's there.

Despite the lavish display there are no hearts of the sort I imagine. Sold out or simply not made anymore. The memory of an Elvis Presley heart rises before me – the singer's blue-black tousle of hair and pulpy snarl surrounded by red satin. What longing I have for such an over-the-top valentine! I told my husband I didn't want chocolate this year – but suddenly wonder why something as important as the giving and receiving of hearts should depend so much on words. Such are my thoughts as I prowl through Wegmans with bits of ash on my forehead while trying to find something pulsing red and sweet.

I turn toward prepared foods, passing savory items packaged in heart-shaped tins: shrimp looking like fleshy pink commas; scallops with garlic sauce; massive rib eyes; butter from a creamery in France. The bakery is a circus of whipped cream and sugar. Macarons keep company with mousses and elegant fruit tarts. Chocolate-covered strawberries are offered beside cut-out cookies and deconstructed cannoli with tubs of sweetened ricotta for dipping. There are cheesecakes, chocolate tortes, and almond cookies by the pound. Boxed pączki and king cakes sit on a table to one side, leftovers from Mardi Gras.

A few shoppers pass by with blackened crosses on their heads and I feel guilty for wiping most of mine away. It's always this way. I stand in line for ashes, then smudge them into my hairline as soon as I leave church. I think of the self-consciousness I seem to have been born with and remember high school where you could pay fifty cents to have a flower delivered to someone's homeroom on Valentine's Day. Red or pink carnations; sometimes white with scarlet striations. We sent them to each other, sisters and crushes and friends, but even a bunch of city kids knew carnations were nothing like roses, which could be dried and saved. I hoist a flat of overpriced water into my grocery cart and try to gauge how much I'd pay for one of those carnations now. I think of all the things held at bay over the years: the tacky, the common, the cheap – how perfect they are, I realize, and I'm flooded with the memory of construction paper hearts, trimmed with doilies, thick with sweet-smelling paste. How to make sense of it all – Ash Wednesday's proscriptions and the grocery store, mad with Valentine's desire? The question returns me to November, to Albuquerque, and the most beautiful skeleton in the world.

We'd scored a prime spot on the concrete island on Isleta Boulevard by showing up hours before the thousands of others who would come. I stood with my friend Giannine in Albuquerque's South Valley waiting for the *Muertos y Marigolds* (Death and Marigolds) Parade. When the sun began to burn, I leapt to the other side of the road, taking refuge in a shaded spot near a group of girls in black T-shirts printed with rib cages, and leggings featuring femurs and tibias. Flowers bloomed from their eye sockets and the points of their chins. A girl held a sugar skull to her mouth and bit into it with her baby teeth. The South Valley was full of skeletons that day.

They glided past on roller skates, skateboards and scooters; passed on stilts, bicycles and flatbeds. Skeleton brides held hands with skeleton cowboys; skeletons in peasant dresses kept company with skeletons in woven ponchos and sombreros. A *Virgen de Guadalupe* wore a gold-trimmed mantle and a halo of scarlet mums. A storm trooper's mask was painted into an elaborate skull. There were chubby skeletons and bony skeletons; baby skeletons and senior citizen skeletons; white skeletons and black skeletons and Mexican skeletons – but the skeleton to beat all skeletons was the boy with marigolds behind his ears.

The marigold is known as *flor de muertos*; its bright petals and pungent scent are said to guide spirits back home on *Día de los Muertos* (Day of the Dead). Because the Mexican holiday is observed on the same days as Halloween, All Saints Day, and All Souls Day, it's often mistaken as an amalgam of the three. While there's some cultural overlap, *Día de los Muertos* is rooted in the pre-Catholic tradition of celebrating the dead. The holiday doesn't simply acknowledge the dead, but makes an active place for them in our lives. Customized altars display photographs of the deceased, along with their favorite objects and best-loved foods. Families come to cemeteries with music and decorate the graves with candles and flowers and glitter. If Tía Consolación was a knitter and an avid fan of sopapillas, you might find a ball of yarn and a jar of honey on her grave, as well as a glass of water and a shot of tequila to quench her thirst after the long journey home.

Volunteers had distributed marigolds before the parade began. I'd crossed back into the sun by then and wondered what do with the tiny flowers and gangly stems. My skin was burning, and I felt sluggish from the oversized horchata I'd gulped. I brushed the hair from my forehead and considered tossing the flowers aside. That's when I noticed the boy. In jeans and a red plaid shirt, he sat beside his mother and little brother on the curb across the street, their brown faces painted into simple white skulls. Seven or eight years old, the boy had plucked the gold florets from the stems and stuck the yellow flowers behind his ears, then helped his brother do the same. Everyone around him fidgeted, our impatience escalating every minute the parade was delayed. We shifted our weight, checked our phones, and shaded our eyes while staring in the direction from which the parade was set to come while the boy sat on the curb lifting his skull-face to the sun.

When the parade finally began, he clapped at faded blue Chevy pickups covered in tissue-paper flowers and strings of chili peppers and garlands of plastic skulls. He raised his hands to the marching band, directing musicians with spider webs glittering on their cheeks. His eyes went wide as lowriders equipped with hydraulics showed off, the slick Bel Air and Impala with fins hopping up and down. The boy scrambled for candy thrown from floats, bounced his head to English songs and Spanish songs, and cheered at the line of decorated vw buses – even when one stalled and had to be pushed along Isleta Boulevard, the little skeleton smiled the entire time, marigolds trumpeting from his ears.

The day before the Marigold Parade, we'd driven to Santa Fe, then taken the scenic road through Chimayó to Taos. The aspens were gold against the Sangre de Cristo mountains. At Chimayó we stopped at *El Santuario*. The shrine's fence line was woven with rosaries, photographs, and pink plastic flowers. Roughly hewn crosses were nailed to trees with larger crosses set into corners and stacked against outbuildings. These were left as offerings by the thousands of pilgrims who come during Holy Week – most walk thirty miles from Santa Fe, while the more fervent travel ninety miles from Albuquerque by foot. The shrine is famous for its holy dirt (*tierra bendita*), which is said to cure everything from arthritis to chronic exhaustion and pervasive sadness. Some pilgrims run their hands through the soil and sprinkle it on their arms and faces, though a flyer warns us not to eat it. So many people come to Chimayó that the pit of holy dirt requires constant refilling. In the old days the caretakers claimed the hole was miraculously refilled, but these days they admit to replenishing it with soil from nearby hills.

Inside the simple adobe church a side room is marked with a sign: *Holy Dirt Room*. Also called *El Pocito* or the Well, the room is so small only a few go in at a time and must duck to step in and out. We wait our turn as the sound of Mass leaks in from the chapel next door. An opening in the planked door offers a view of the altar and I watch the line of faces arriving for Communion. *Receive the Body of Christ*, the priest says. *Amen* comes the response. *Amen. Amen. Amen.* As regular and rhythmic as breath, the responses provide a backbeat as people shuffle in and out of the Holy Dirt Room using sandbox-style shovels to scoop it into envelopes and old pill bottles.

We'd stopped by the gift shop on the way in and listened as the girl near the register told stories of cures. Giannine asked questions and bought a container for dirt while I looked at a wall of *retablos* and bought one of the Virgin and a few plastic rosaries to leave at the shrine.

"Here," I said, offering a rosary to Giannine.

"I don't know what I believe," she said, and neither did I. But I'd noticed the way she'd listened as the young woman talked about the possibilities of the sacred dirt.

"Just leave one and think of someone," I said. Her sister had recently died. A young woman with small children. The cancer had arrived unannounced and torn through her body in a matter of weeks.

Now we step into the dirt room. Framed prints of the saints are strung with medals and plastic flowers. A few statues occupy a corner. Our Lady. The Holy Infant of Atocha. Saint Jude with a pile of coins in the crook of his peeling arm.

I scoop a bit of dirt into my gift shop bag and leave the room to listen to the final bits of Mass while waiting for Giannine. I remember the way leaves had blazed as we drove north and the stand of cottonwoods so yellow I'd pulled over and stood beneath their brilliant skirts. I think of the framed photographs on an altar in Santa Fe's *Santuario de Guadalupe*, the collection of black and white faces surrounded by candles and mums.

Why should it be so surprising, this pairing of death and flowers? When did we split the world into opposing categories and allow for maximum doses of one while attempting to keep the other under wraps? We long for flowers and chocolate but will take rain checks on the ashes and dust. And why not? It's natural to be less inclined toward soil than roses. The only problem is that it's a lie, this divide. There are no roses without soil.

How little it matters that the pit is refilled by human hands. How inconsequential whether the claims of cured limps and restored knees can ever be validated and whether our sadness continues after Chimayó. That the soil is holy I have no doubt. It's constantly dying and being reborn, this sacred heartbreaking world.

We're constantly dying too and rising again. Our lives are a parade of Ash Wednesdays and Valentine's Days, a thousand Good Fridays, a steady stream of Easters and New Year's Eves. Why wouldn't we walk around with ashes on our foreheads and marigolds blooming from our ears?

SEARCH FOR THE VIRGIN, PART VII

Buffalo

Saint Agnes stands in a pale pink robe holding her martyr's palm leaf and cradling a lamb. Even as I shake Mary Holland's hand at the entrance to the Arts Center, my eyes fly to Agnes and the smattering of other figures near the door. This is who you've become, I say to myself, a woman who looks at statues instead of people. After this, I remind myself, you're done. But even as I chide myself and vow reform, I catch sight of an Our Lady of Mt. Carmel, brown robed and exquisitely made. The Corpus Christi Virgin is not likely to be here, I know.

As I drove along the thruway, past snowbanks and salt trucks, I looked toward the sky blanketed by clouds and tried not to overindulge the possibility of finding her. Some combination of superstition and longing-management has caused me to keep such reckless bouts of hope in check over the years. Instead, I marvel at the size of snowbanks with my husband, who has come along, and make a game of trying to calculate the number of Marian statues in this part of the state. The number of outdoor crèches and bathtub grottoes alone boggles the mind. Perhaps that's why I'm so stunned when, just as I'm falling a little in love with the brave and beautiful Agnes, I spy a mantle so blue I know immediately I have found her.

Mary Holland is giving a wonderful tour and the church and its contents are magnificent, but once I see her the words begin to hit my head like snow on a windshield, melting and sliding away. I see only the color of oceans on antique maps, the precise shade of forget-me-nots and certain late winter skies.

She wears no crown and does not stand like a queen on a globe. She's not carved from fine Italian marble or the wood of a single French oak. Her bearing is humble, her expression mild. But how lovely she is. Lovelier than I remember. Lovelier than any image of the Blessed Mother I've ever seen. My husband touches my shoulder as I walk toward her, and though I've spent most of my life trying not to get attached to things that can be lost, I bring my hands to my face in the manner of prayer.

"Hello, Mary," I say. *Hello sweet Lady.*

14

A Brief History of Prayer

Stands of southern pine divide the highway south of Richmond. Fields are frosted. Breath becomes fog at the rest stop. The sun comes up near the Carolina border, as license plate mottos change from *Virginia Is for Lovers* to *First in Flight*. Semis rumble past carrying logs. The air smells of burning wood. I pass signs for peanuts and tobacco and a forty-foot fiberglass statue of Paul Bunyan and his blue ox Babe, and read a series of billboards: *One in Five Children Faces Hunger. Gentlemen's Playground. Actors, Models, & Talent for Christ.*

My clothes are packed and stored neatly on the back seat. I sip coffee and listen to music, and everything's fine until a few miles north of Rocky Mount, when the idea of the ocean enters my head. I'm on my way to a monastery near Atlanta for a retreat, but what does the ocean care for such details? It unfolds like an unwieldy map, and once it's open I can't fold it back. I try to sing over it, and when that doesn't work I imagine the wise things the monks will say and remind myself of the baked goods advertised on their website – the delicate biscotti and fruitcake packed with pecans and dried cherries. *The baking is overseen by Father Augustine,* the description read, *who soaks the cakes in sherry and peach brandy.* I see the monks at work in a simple but well-stocked kitchen, a gentle Father Augustine perpetually stirring batter. The image manages to distract me for a few minutes, but it turns out that even sherry-soaked cake can keep the ocean at bay for only so long.

Recalculating route, the GPS says as I exit 95 and head east on 64. I reach over and turn off the navigation. The sun is full force now. I can hardly see where I'm going for all the light. Flocks of tundra swans rest off the highway, the large white birds lending elegance to bedraggled winter ponds. I stop for more coffee in Tarboro, call the retreat center to let them know I'm not coming, then check a map to see where I'm headed exactly. Roanoke. Nag's Head. The northern stretch of the Outer Banks.

Back on the road, the terrain flattens into cypress swamps and solar farms. Signs begin to advertise seafood and beachfront hotels. Near the Scuppernong River a billboard with an image of a smiling African child: *You Can Change a Life.*

Thérèse of Lisieux believed prayer was *a surge of the heart, a cry of recognition and of love, embracing both trial and joy.*

Talk to Him just like you're sitting here talking to me, my friend Mary advises. *He doesn't need fancy words. He just likes to hear your voice.*

I do not know You God because I am in the way, Flannery O'Connor wrote. *Please help me to push myself aside.*

I listen to them equally, Flannery and Mary and Saint Thérèse, but relate more to Wendell Berry, who described prayer as being like *a bird that has blundered down the flue and is caught indoors and flutters at the windowpanes.*

My own prayer began in earnest last year. I'd said prayers since I was a child, but it was mainly the mouthing of words and, as much as I'd liked church, prayer never came easily. It seemed to me a private thing, quiet and close to the body. But in the past year what had been largely theoretical suddenly came alive for me – the sabbatical that had provided nearly a year to rediscover my childhood church had spent itself; I was in a new city starting a new job at a new university; my marriage had shaped itself more fully into a question mark.

The pain did not descend full force until I landed in Virginia. I set a tiny statue of a sleeping Joseph on my nightstand. The statue came from a trip to Rome with my sister a few months before. I'd scoured gift shops near the Vatican after reading that Pope Francis wrote down his problems on slips of paper, then folded and placed them under the sleeping Joseph's head, letting the saint work things out while the pontiff slept. Now, in desperation, I did the same. *Where am I headed?* I scribbled. *Help me know what to do.*

Dear God, I said before I fell asleep. The word God was still awkward to me – but there I was, attempting to speak it as though we were old friends. The words sounded forced and distant. Like trying to sing full-throated melodies through a hollow reed. But I kept on. *Dear God*, I said. Again and again, hoping it would take.

A year later I still had more questions than answers, but the sharpest edges of pain had passed. My attempt at prayer was a habit by then but had not lost its tinny sound. I was facing a birthday and trying to decide on appropriately festive plans when I saw the retreat advertised at the Monastery of the Holy Spirit near Atlanta. *Have I actually forgotten how to have fun?* I wondered when I chose a retreat called Prayer and the Image of God instead of drinks with friends or a weekend with my husband to celebrate. *What kind of person does that?* I thought and the answer came flashing back: *You do, and for now it's going to have to be okay.*

When the day came I packed plain clothes, which are, in truth, the only kind of clothes I own. I packed a toothbrush and face cream, and, though I feared it would mark me as too worldly, slipped a blow dryer into the pillowcase left behind from my sister's visit the summer before, a soft rectangle of cloth covered with moons and stars that my youngest nephew had used back when he was new.

At Roanoke a man at the Visitor Center points to a map of the Outer Banks.

"Some of the lighthouses and boardwalks are closed for winter," he says. "Things won't get going again until March."

I've come in to ask about hotels – which will be open and where – but suddenly remember the wild ponies near Corolla. When I ask about them, he corrects my pronunciation.

"Cah-rah-la," he says, and shows me the place where the road ends and the beach to the ponies begins. "Not far from where I grew up."

He motions to a town called Duck and laughs when I ask if he still lives there. "It was only a few houses without running water when I was a child but that was nearly eighty years ago – it's all million-dollar houses now."

"Let me show you something," he says, and even before he opens the brochure I catch sight of the Wright brothers and grimace inside. I've never been much interested in the history of flight. He spreads the brochure between us and points to grainy photographs of a biplane surrounded by shadowy figures who'd come out to see the brothers from Ohio try to get their flyer into the sky.

"December 17, 1903," he says. "Their first successful flight."

"This one," he brings out another photograph, "is a few days before they flew."

The wash of light mutes the features of those surrounding the plane and makes them into ghosts. Six silhouettes, four men and two boys. All face the camera except the smallest, who looks up and into his father's face while holding onto his hand.

"My daddy." My visitor center friend touches the child with the tip of his finger; his fingernail halos the boy's head. "And that's his daddy there, and their dog."

The photograph is 114 years old, but I can feel the retriever panting on the sand.

"The brothers didn't make it into the sky that day," he says. "But Daddy knew they would."

When did it begin, the desire to connect to that which is larger than but essential to our everyday selves? And how to properly fathom when it began when the action of prayer itself is so unclear? Is it pleading or praise or bouts of intentionally sitting still? Is it a way to flag down God's attention? An attempt to channel him? A spell to sway her our way?

Maybe it started with Eve. Laboring under a hut of branches, child tearing from her flesh. *What is this thing?* she thought while biting down on strips of bark and longing for something like a mother. But there were no mothers. Also not invented: sisters, midwives, friends. She'd have to give birth to all of this herself. Until then there was only Adam, wringing his hands and bringing her water from time to time. They'd have watched the animals closely over the past few months. When Eve's stomach began to swell, they'd have told themselves it was like what happened with the rabbits and gazelles and the foxes. But how could they be sure? *God*, she would have screamed. *God.* Until the child emerged – the shock of black hair followed by a pair of shoulders folded in like wings. Like nothing they'd ever seen. Still, they somehow knew to cut him loose and set him to her chest, the mess of his body settling into her own.

It might have started the moment Adam first saw Eve. Her legs wobbled as she tried to stand and he rushed over to brace her while rubbing the sleep from his own eyes – and perhaps because one of his bones had been recently stolen, the cage over his heart had loosened and freed up space for the first prayer to launch from his still-tender chest.

Or else it was just after they'd left Eden, the loss so profound, it reshaped their cells so dramatically it was replicated onto our own – making the space between the human body and Paradise a gap we still ache to close. How blue the sky had been. How lovingly their Maker had fashioned the clouds for their enjoyment. Enormous wispy things. Smiling tigers. A line of cherubs. Airships with seventeen varieties of sails. All of this, until they were shown the door. But no, I suppose they would have been too agog for prayer. So stunned by rejection, they could only make their eyes into saucers while holding tight to their fig leaves. Only after the path they'd come from had closed behind them did they understand how very lost and free they were. Then, perhaps, Eve extended her hand to Adam. Then, perhaps, Adam reached back. The moment their flesh connected in the new and imperfect world: one might call this prayer.

In my hotel room I open the curtains to a view of the ocean but the door to the balcony is stuck. I lie back on the bed and close my eyes. A wave of loneliness washes through me. That being alone is exactly what I'd wanted makes it no easier to bear. I think of my husband, the fine hikes he would have led wherever we'd met, the perfect cake he would have baked. I imagine others arriving at the monastery and wonder what I'm missing at the retreat.

I see them then – a group of people closing their eyes and following a guided meditation. The late evening sun streams through the windows. And while I somehow understand that monks don't bring snacks to prayer sessions, I let myself imagine the brothers doling out fruitcake. I see the retreatants bringing slices to their mouths and think just then of the friend I did not make. The one who wears flat shoes like I do, who laughs easily and can't help herself from nipping another crumble of cake as one of the brothers quotes John Chrysostom:

> The potency of prayer hath subdued the strength of fire; it hath bridled the rage of lions, hushed anarchy to rest, extinguished wars, appeased the elements, expelled demons, burst the chains of death, expanded the gates of heaven, assuaged diseases, repelled frauds, rescued cities from destruction, stayed the sun in its course, and arrested the progress of the thunderbolt.

The retreatants are smiling now, made placid and full by the cake and the loftiness of the quote. I'm smiling too, imagining prayer powerful enough to halt thunderbolts. Like Charlton Heston parting the Technicolor sea. Like the kind of prayer I grew up with, where the goal was to convince God to lower a divine hand into our lives and mix things up a bit so that circumstances might more favorably align. I enjoy the possibility, and, while my life could use some reshuffling, I understand that what most requires stirring are the circumstances of my own heart. One of the monks digs deeper into his bag of quotes and finds another, this one by Abraham Heschel:

Prayer may not save us, he winks. *But prayer may make us worthy of being saved.*

It's late January, but people still come to the shore.

In the morning I walk on the beach and watch two children chasing waves.

The sky is milky and, with the sun coming out, the family is in silhouette. I think of the man at the Visitor Center and his father at six years old standing beside the magnificent machine on the towering dunes. Beyond him the Alligator River. In the other direction the Atlantic. The Wright brothers had contemplated flying for years. They'd consumed every book on the subject and scrutinized the movement of birds, experimenting with kites and gliders and wings. They were convinced human flight was possible and for this endured ridicule and, even worse, their own doubt. But they kept on, year after year, and eventually came to Kill Devil Hills to practice gliding. Again and again. Hundreds of times. This was their secret. Others pursuing flight focused on the airplane itself, but the brothers understood that even the best machine required a navigator who knew how to fly.

They chose the Outer Banks for the steady winds, the isolation, and the large dunes, which made for soft landings. Perhaps that's why I've come too. I drive along the Virginia Dare Trail and Highway 12, visiting beaches from Hatteras to Currituck.

Colossal pastel houses block the ocean for stretches, but the view west opens to marshes, fishing piers, and the sound.

At Nag's Head I stare into the ocean and collect broken shells whose claret undersides make them look like rose petals in the sand. I hear a sound down the beach and can't tell if it's crying or laughter or the squawking of a gull. How alike the sounds of pain and joy are, I realize. How little need I have these days to parse them out.

On the morning of December 17, 1903, the Wright brothers walked onto the dunes wearing coats and ties as if headed to church. The air was chilly. The previous day's weather had been perfect, but it was Sunday and they refused to try on the Sabbath. They were decidedly not religious, the strange brothers with the flat Ohio accents, but that did not mean they were not reverent.

Wilbur had made the first attempt the Friday before, after returning from a trip back to Dayton to repair and replace broken propeller shafts. He lifted off from the slope of Big Kill Devil Hill, but the motor stalled out after a few seconds. Now it's Monday of the week before Christmas, and the weather is turning. They must try today or lose the chance. At 10:35 Orville climbs into the flyer and up it goes. The sun burns off the mist as the flying machine rises into the air. He hovers above the earth for twelve fat seconds. Later that day Wilbur will stay up for nearly a minute, and Orville will fly again, staying airborne longer still.

Orville took his father up seven years later, in May of 1910. He helped his father into the plane and took off from Huffman Prairie in Dayton. They stayed up for seven full minutes. A bishop in the United Brethren of Christ Church, the elder Wright had stocked his home with books full of questions. A man who'd dedicated himself to doctrine, he had not required the same of his children and once brought his boys a toy helicopter from his travels.

Higher, Orville! The eighty-two-year old bishop shouted. *Higher!*

I trudge through the dunes, listening to warblers in the scrub pines.

I see the boy again. His panting dog. And, more than a century later, his son handing out Visitor Center brochures. The impossibility of it all. Gone now: the ultra-rational brothers who seemed to have loved nothing (no woman, no God, no vice) so much as the prospect of flight. Gone now: their preacher father, soaring over Huffman Prairie. Gone now: the little boy holding onto his father's hand.

Only his son's words linger: *That's my Daddy.* And the sound of those words in an old man's mouth, the soft tug of them filtered through a coastal Carolina voice, just about undoes me. *Dear God*, I say most nights, and though they don't yet glide, my words, I think they someday will.

On my last night I lie back and listen to the ocean. I've traded the Trappists, their boozy fruitcake, and monastery for the Outer Banks, but can't fully let them go. I imagine them rising for Lauds and coming together for a simple and silent breakfast.

What a fine retreat it's been, everyone says. *And what perfect leaders.* The good brothers smile in gratitude and, just as the retreatants say goodbye and begin to slip one at a time out the door, the friend I didn't make quotes Simone Weil: *Even if our efforts seem for years to be producing no result, one day a light in their exact proportion will flood the soul.*

And like a priest imparting a blessing, she lifts her hand into the air, pulls back the curtain of distance and time, finds me in my oceanfront Holiday Inn, and once again quotes Weil: *Attention is prayer.*

I believe I've been shortsighted in assuming that prayer requires a human body to convey it or that prayer amounts to the saying of anything at all. Maybe it's not speaking so much as listening, and not listening so much as quieting ourselves enough to fall back into the space before words. It's possible that prayer began before any of us, or was, in fact, our beginning. Perhaps we are, each of us, litanies of clay and breath.

And what about the earliest days? Stars set into blackness, glittering long before human eyes ever lit upon them; the ocean filled with magnificent creatures, the tide scattering shells. Was that not prayer? Or is a singular beating heart required? The first bird then. A raven or a catbird. The night heron maybe, or the tiniest of songbirds. A ruby-crowned kinglet, let's say. Not the moment it was fashioned, each feather of its exquisite head teased into a hundred scarlet fronds, each bone chiseled into existence. That was something, yes. But prayer requires circumstances larger than the individual. Perhaps it wasn't the making of the bird, then, but the moment it found itself in the wide blue sky and without thinking opened its wings.

15

Feast of the Epiphany

The girl strokes the dove with one of her thumbs. The bird may have resisted her hands initially but has acclimated to its perch and surveys the crowd with a beady pink eye. Each year a different girl is chosen to carry the dove in the procession from St. Nicholas Cathedral to Spring Bayou. The teen wears a lace-trimmed robe over her dress and a simple Greek cross around her neck. Ribbons cascade from her cupped hands, making a waterfall tail for the bird. Inside the cathedral the congregation is dressed to the nines – everyone except the rows of high school boys wearing "Epiphany 2018" T-shirts and swim trunks.

A few blocks away, Craig Park is already packed. Lawn chairs are set onto the sloped lawns and paved walkway circling the bayou. Blankets and coolers are spread under live oaks whose branches drip Spanish moss. A manatee appears in the water every few minutes, its tremendous backside surfacing as it turns. Fourteen thousand people have come to Tarpon Springs this year – fewer than expected because of the severe blizzard that's canceled flights up and down the East Coast. The day began hours ago for those in the cathedral with 8 a.m. prayers and Divine Liturgy followed by the Great Blessing of the Waters at noon. Those in Craig Park missed all this. Epiphany may be a religious feast, but most have come to this small Florida city to see the boys dive into the bayou.

As I wait for the procession to begin, I listen to chanting unfurling from a loudspeaker near the cathedral. The Greek Orthodox liturgy sounds exotic and faraway – like the soaring human voice in the Islamic call to prayer braided with strands of the Roman Mass and incense smoke. I sip coffee and stand in a patch of sun outside the church, waiting for the procession to begin.

"Happy Epiphany!" The man on a street corner holds a sign proclaiming the need to repent and be saved. The radio beside him blares evangelical hymns. His music is outmatched by the cathedral loudspeaker, but coupled with the sign seems an act of minor aggression.

"Happy Epiphany," I say back.

The street preacher is one of the few shouting greetings in English. Tarpon Springs is home to the largest percentage of Greeks in the United States, and Greek is the language of choice today.

Chrónia Pollá! says a father with two young children as he passes.

Chrónia Pollá! A clutch of women returns the holiday greeting. In their midsixties or so, they link arms and laugh as they push down Pinellas Avenue. Two men drinking coffee at an outside table could have been lifted from an Athens street scene. At the hotel coffee stand this morning, greetings of *Kaliméra* outranked *Good Morning* two to one. Locals burrow under hats and down coats while those from more northerly locations wear spring jackets. A few even brave sandals and shorts. Welcome to Florida in early January, where the region you've flown in from dictates how cold or warm you will feel. This January is chillier than most, with deep freezes as far south as Tallahassee. There are reports of iguanas so cold they've fallen from trees. Leave them be, the articles advise; they can be unpredictable when they thaw.

Sometime after noon the procession begins. Children parade by in Greek *fustanellas* and pom-pom shoes, followed by dancers in folk dresses and veils. The dove bearer walks beside last year's winning diver, who holds a massive trophy in his hands. This year's Epiphany divers march by, all new muscle and bare feet. An icon of the baptism of Jesus is surrounded by flowers and displayed in a carved box hoisted onto seminarians' shoulders. Girls in white dresses are tethered to the box with long ribbons and encircle it like a maypole. Altar boys carry censers and candles, lanterns and ornate liturgical fans. Next come the clerics: priests, deacons, and subdeacons – all in gold cloaks – followed by the Metropolitan of Atlanta. Layered in richly embroidered vestments, the bishop wears a brocade crown studded with gemstones and a series of small icons. With his white beard and crozier, he looks like a solemn but gilded Santa Claus.

Once they reach Craig Park, the bishop stands on a raised platform overlooking the water as the boys – fifty-seven this year – swim out to a semicircle of boats. It's the size of a small lake, the rounded end of Spring Bayou. As is customary in the Orthodox tradition, the bishop blesses the local body of water with a Holy Cross, which he will throw in and the swimmers compete to retrieve. The winner will be celebrated and is said to be blessed for a whole year.

The boys climb onto the gunwales as the bishop blesses the bayou with a clump of fresh basil and a priest chants the story of Christ's baptism. Those who'd been inside the church for five hours must have to summon their patience, but the sound of prayer is new to the people in the park, who look up from their lawn chairs and don't seem to mind how long it goes on. Eventually the sign is given. The girl opens her hands and the dove flies overhead as the bishop tosses a scalloped white cross into the bayou. The boys plunge in. Everyone cheers as the great ruckus and foam give way to the sight of heads bobbing in the water. The boys go under again and again in search of the cross. After a few minutes a boy shouts out, victorious, and looks like a young Marlon Brando as he's first blessed by the Metropolitan, then lifted onto shoulders and taken up by the crowd.

The sight of young men leaping into the bayou is strangely moving. I did not expect my breath to catch as I stood under a live oak watching. Even more impressive was the way they'd perched before they jumped, four or five to a boat. They shivered in wet trunks for the duration of the prayers. They must have been at least as tired as the rest of us, but every last boy bent forward the whole time, poised and waiting, everything in him wound up and ready to leap. Spring Bayou is not deep, but as they waited for the bishop to toss the cross all fifty-seven boys looked prepared to jump off the edge of the earth.

Also called Theophany, Epiphany is one of the great feasts of the Orthodox Church and celebrates the visible manifestation of God. The central image is of John the Baptist pouring water over Jesus on the banks of the Jordan while the Holy Spirit descends and God the Father calls out his pleasure from above. In contrast, the Roman Catholic observance of Epiphany celebrates the arrival of the Magi to the infant Jesus – their recognition and adoration of his divinity has become our iconic image. In the early days of the Church, Epiphany also commemorated the baptism of Christ, but Rome eventually assigned the gospel events separate feast days. Perhaps that's why, in much of the United States, Epiphany can seem like a liturgical footnote.

There are homilies inspired by the journey of the wise men, their faith in heading west toward a mysterious light, and the precious gifts they bore. Occasionally local customs mark the day. Father Bob, for instance, invites three parishioners to don robes and crowns and stand with him during Mass – the trio of kingly shadows representing Caspar, Melchior, and Balthazar following his every move. Later he uses chalk to bless the church with an inscription of the Magi's initials (20+C+M+B+18), which hover like an ecclesiastical math problem over the lintel.

Certain cultural groups also embrace the day. Growing up, my Puerto Rican friends left out grass for the Magi's camels on *El Día de los Reyes* (Three Kings Day) and were rewarded with small gifts. Along parts of the Gulf Coast people eat King Cake to mark the start of Mardi Gras season, and, around the country, Epiphany is often used as a marker to take down holiday lights, garlands, and trees. But, outside of the Magi in their nativity sets or a homily at church, most American Catholics do not consider the kings at all and Epiphany is a quiet day. Perhaps that's why I love it.

I like the word itself, and the way that, in a literary sense, it's come to stand for culminations of sound and image – bursts of revelation conveyed by what seems, at first glance, a sort of beautiful gibberish. I also enjoy how, in a larger sense, the word refers to those unexpected flashes of meaning and light most of us have experienced, and the way that – whether it celebrates Jesus's baptism or a group of Seers following a faraway star – Epiphany celebrates the manifestation of the divine. It's a sort of hushed Christmas. The pomp and bang of the winter holidays with all the glitter and expectation is gone. The air is still. Northern fields are covered with snow. Just as the world gathers itself back into the grind, resuming its steady forward chug, here comes a day to remind us of leaps of faith and little awakenings awaiting us all.

Maybe that's why I decided to travel to the place that calls itself Epiphany City. Even as I'd relearned my prayers and had once again fallen in love with the Mass, heading back to church remained a shock to my system and I still struggled to understand what propelled me there. Why head back to the same church most everyone I knew had abandoned, especially when there were such compelling reasons for leaving? Why swim in the opposite direction of the stream? Such questions sent me to Tarpon Springs. What might happen, I wondered, in such a place?

Back in Tarpon Springs the crowd splits up after the Epiphany dive. The boys dry off in special edition–printed Epiphany towels, and, after a series of blessings and photographs, return with their families to the St. Nicholas courtyard for food and dancing. The less religiously inclined head out for meals of dolmades and crab-stuffed grouper at one of the *tavernas*, followed by baklava and Greek coffee. Later they'll stroll the sponge docks, traipsing past palm trees strung with lights, walking into souvenir shops laden with baskets of sand dollars and dried alligator heads; conch and lightning whelk shells; and all manner of sea sponges. Once the city's bread and butter, sponge diving is what originally brought Greeks to the city back in 1905. The sponge industry grew quickly, and within a few years two thousand Greek divers had arrived, fishing so successfully along the Anclote River and the Florida Gulf that, long before it was known as Epiphany City, Tarpon Springs was called the Sponge Capital of the World.

The industry came to a halt when the sponge beds died out and the synthetic version was developed, but the Greek influence remains. A plywood warrior towers over the Hellas Bakery, complete with Corinthian helmet, *hoplon*, and spear. A mural on the corner of Hope Street and Dodecanese features a diver in a portaled metal helmet – like something out of Jules Verne, an underwater spaceman with a mermaid hovering over his right shoulder. A boat laden with sponges looks like those I've seen in the Aegean – which makes sense, since most local Greek families emigrated from the same region whose island economies depended for centuries on sponge fishing.

Said to be the best in the world, before modern diving equipment existed Greek divers leapt into the ocean with only rope and a thirty-pound marble slab. Known as a *skandalopetra*, the stone propelled the diver into the depths, where he cut away sponges, deposited them into a net, then yanked the rope to be pulled back to the surface by its tender – all while holding his breath. This is the tradition the boys who jumped into the bayou descended from. These are the stories told and retold around grandmothers' tables. Great-grandfathers and uncles who held smooth flat stones to their chests, said silent prayers, then tumbled into the sea.

Though tempted by the prospect of bakeries, I decide against the sponge docks and trail the crowd heading back to the cathedral. I walk up the steps, make a donation, and take a bundle of white tapers. The church is all light and arches and Byzantine murals. Icons strung with votive offerings and vigil lanterns decorate one side of the sanctuary. Crystal chandeliers hang from the ceiling and the altar is fashioned of Greek marble, but even with its lavish trimmings the domed cathedral seems elegant and spare. I follow the line of people shuffling past an icon of Saint Nicholas, which is said to weep, walk through the church, and eventually end up back where I started in the narthex near the candle stand. An older Greek woman watches as people light their tapers, bow their heads, and move on. Most hand the tiny woman their candles to place in the sand-filled stand. Hundreds of candles burn, with a nonstop line of people waiting to add more. The woman is needed, I see, to manage the limited plot of space.

I light the tapers and hand a few her way, but keep two to place on my own. I can feel the line shifting behind me and do not like to hold them up, but when will I ever stand in this place again? I look into the lit candles and think of the boys in swimming trunks and the legions of divers who came before them. I think of my unexpected return to church, which I'd accepted and come to see as a gift, even as I struggled to understand. As I place a candle in the stand, I imagine a cool flat stone fitting itself to my chest. A *skandalopetra*, like the ones old-time divers used to propel themselves to the depths. It's suddenly clear to me – with all the worrying and weighing and wondering – how cautiously I've proceeded on this journey back to church. I'd delighted in Epiphany and admired the bravery of the wise men for as long as I can remember, but in my own approach I've barely gotten my feet wet.

Faith – like jumping into a bayou or hopping on a camel and following a faraway star – can't be done halfway. It's not so much what you believe as what you do with those beliefs, and it is called faith precisely because it doesn't make sense. You must be daring and a little reckless and occasionally abandon the overused helmet of your head. And just as there's no perfect time to tumble into the ocean or to leave the comfort of home in search of a mysterious source of light, there is no perfect church. There is no perfect spouse or family or anything really – which is why devotion cannot depend on circumstance. I understand this, at least in theory – but how often have I scrutinized others, found myself disappointed, and used that disappointment as an excuse to succumb to the waxy spell of indifference and my finely honed capacity for walking away?

The line behind me once again tenses. The candle lady narrows her eyes, as if trying to fathom how a person can be so slow in the lighting and placement of tapers. But on this holy Feast of Epiphany in the city of Epiphany this is my moment of epiphany. I'm standing inside St. Nicholas, yes, but I'm not only placing candles. I'm listening too. Can't she hear it? The chanting over the water? The sudden flutter of wings? The thumping inside our chests? Doesn't she see the way we are, each of us, perched and waiting on the edge of a boat?

SEARCH FOR THE VIRGIN, PART VIII

Rochester

"So did you bring her home?"

The question comes without fail when I tell people about the search.

It's possible the asker doesn't realize the statue's dimensions and imagines I might pop her into a tote bag and convey her to my desk. Or they understand her dimensions but assume someone with such statue fever would have arranged for a few men and a pickup. Maybe the only way my quest makes sense is if it results in a measurable endpoint – some tangible outcome to justify the search itself. But there's no justification wide enough to explain the nameless thing that descends at various points in our lives and demands movement. *Go*, something whispers. *Go*.

By the time I found my Mary, I'd accepted that practicality is not the only guidepost in our lives. While her mantle remains the truest shade of blue I've ever seen and I could look into it for years, I'd already done so for half of my life. The search was never about trying to return her to the church that had let her go. In fact, the opposite was true. It turns out that while I'm pretty good at slipping away, I'm quite slow when it comes to letting go. It had taken a few decades and a multicity search to better appreciate what I'd once had – and, by extension, what I'd lost.

Corpus Christi was a beacon of beauty and light in a community that desperately needed both. I want to believe that such spaces will be saved, especially in neighborhoods that can no longer support them. I hope we'll find ways to safeguard these sanctuaries in our own cities, and perhaps even heat them with the warmth of our bodies from time to time. But for all my wishing otherwise, the community I grew up in is essentially gone. As I drove from church to church looking for Mary, I kept my eyes open for traces of the vibrant tradition I once knew. Instead, I was typically surrounded by a handful of other worshippers, with parishioners and priests well into their golden years and those in both camps often looking uninspired as they repeated the series of motions that had guided their bodies all their lives. If the statue of Our Lady is a symbol of the tradition I was born into, the fact that she's housed in a museum is telling. The dynamic brand of Catholicism that once provided such nourishment is gasping for breath.

The problems in the Church are undeniable. I do not let my appreciation for tradition blind me to its abuses and faults, but neither do I let my anger and disappointment rob me of its riches. The aspects of Catholicism that sustain me are rooted in teachings more vital than the institution that houses it – and it's the institution that's dusty, the institution that's in peril, the institution that must be renewed if it's ever again to thrive.

While I somehow found my Lady – and here my friend Mary Engels would interrupt to be sure proper credit is given to Saint Anthony – looking for her helped me to understand that although the people and places that matter most are flawed – often maddeningly so – this need not sway my concern for them. Devotion is less about where it's bestowed than the disposition of the one who does the bestowing. As much as I cherish the church and its people, I sometimes wonder if where I returned was as important as the fact that I returned to anything at all.

Devotion alone may not translate to transformation – certainly many swaddle themselves in ritual in lieu of a more challenging or dynamic spirituality. But it's equally true that many of us have been too quick to dismiss it as an essential entry point in our attempt to build meaningful lives. No matter what you call it – dedication, commitment, sacrifice – it boils down to loving someone or something other than ourselves, often against reason, so much that we're willing to set personal preferences aside. This does not mean submitting to tyrants or fanaticism or blindly following massive unthinking crowds. It requires nuance and patience and the capacity to withstand doubt. It must be given willingly and decided for ourselves.

This is the legacy of Corpus Christi. The men and women who left mothers in Palermo and uncles in Limerick to cross oceans to try for better lives built thousands of churches in their adopted cities of Syracuse and Pittsburgh and Buffalo. They woke early to help lay the bricks with their own hands before going off to work full days in railroad yards or building canals. They broke themselves, in some cases, to build the same churches that now sit empty or have become condominiums or weedy lots. Sad, yes. Heartbreaking even. But it took a search for a statue to help me see that their devotion wasn't about bricks or even doctrine so much as their ability to look beyond individual concerns toward the common good. It was about creating spaces in which they could come together to elevate and consecrate the ordinary life.

So while I will always have a soft spot for the gentle Lady I looked to before I could even talk – on Sunday, I'll return to the church on the corner of East Main and Prince Streets. The pews will not be crowded. The stone exterior will have darkened; the fixtures may be in need of repair. The faces I once loved will have mostly disappeared. I may feel, at some point, like turning around and walking out the door. Instead, I'll sing a psalm and rise with others for Communion. Instead, I'll approach the right-side altar and stand before Our Lady of Mt. Carmel. Instead, I'll bring match to candle and make a little light right there.

ACKNOWLEDGMENTS

The most wondrous aspects of these journeys were the generous human beings I met along the way. *Merci mille fois à* Father Michael Champagne and Sisters Francesca DuPre and Jeanne d'Arc in St. Martinville. Thank you to Mary Holland at the Buffalo Religious Arts Center, Rosemary at Assumption Church in Buffalo, Mike and Jason Osella at Used Church Items in Pittsburgh, Ann Coughlin in Cork for the trip to Ballinspittle, and Giannine Lioi, fellow pilgrim to New Mexico. Thank you to the Diocese of Buffalo and the Diocese of Rochester, with special gratitude to Sister Connie Derby for access to the archives and to Deb Housel for the lead on the statue of Our Lady. Thank you to James Sarkis for the meticulous record of Rochester churches, to Diamond Auble for fielding my questions, and to Father Jim Callan and Margaret Wittman for sharing Spiritus Christi archives and memories. Thank you to Sister Bernarde Entress for leading the pilgrimage to the shrines of Quebec.

Thank you to Alicia Christensen, the University of Nebraska Press, and the American Lives Series for their tremendous work in ushering diverse stories into the world. Special thanks to Kristen Iversen, Lisa Ampleman, Hattie Fletcher, Katie Brooks, Mary Flinn, Greg Donovan, and the staff and editors who published early versions of these essays. I'm greatly indebted to Sally Parker, Gail Mott, Ann Walton Sieber, Jenny Lloyd, Lee McAvoy, Elizabeth Osta, Gregory Gerard, Justin Maxwell, Peggy Rosenthal, George Dardess, Sally Wood Winslow, and Peter Eckerstrom for their readings, and to Rachel Hall, Gail Hosking, Kristen Gentry, and Sejal Shah for the coffee-fueled writing community. Thank you to Kathryn Thomas and Craig Bullock for inspiration over the years and to John Erb for enthusiasm and insight.

Thank you to Virginia Commonwealth University and the Humanities Research Center for their support of this project, to my colleagues in the English Department, and to my students, who inspire me more than they know.

Thank you to the Sisters of St. Joseph, Sisters of Mercy, School Sisters of Notre Dame, and every unsung sister everywhere. I will never stop thanking Sisters Eileen Daly and Clare Ehmann – that's how much a good teacher can mean.

Tremendous love and gratitude to Mary Engels who inhabits every essay in some way, to Jo Lombardo for helping me back to church, and to Angie Rothert for lending her Communion dress.

I'm ever thankful to and for Fathers William (Mickey) McGrath and Robert T. Werth, past and present parishioners of Corpus Christi/Our Lady of the Americas Church, and the entire community of St. Frances Xavier Cabrini Parish.

Thank you to Jim Mott, trusted reader, partner in wonder, intrepid finder of fireflies.

Thank you to my mother for the gift of the Church.

Early versions of the following essays were published and are reprinted with permission: "Absolute Mystery" in *Creative Nonfiction*; "Feast of Saint Blaise" in *Sojourners*; "Miracle of the Eyes" in the *Cincinnati Review*; "Holy Water" in *Blackbird*; "Act of Contrition," "Search for the Virgin," and "Feast of the Epiphany" in *America* magazine (September 2017, February 2018, and January 2019). A section of "Holy Water" appeared as "Like This We Begin" in *Ruminate* magazine, won the VanderMey Nonfiction Prize, and was listed as notable in *Best American Essays 2018*. "Miracle of the Eyes" was nominated for a Pushcart Prize and selected for inclusion in the 2018 *Orison Anthology*.

SOURCES

AUTHOR'S NOTE

Statistics on declining Catholicism from:

"Pew survey: Percentage of US Catholics Drops and Catholicism Is Losing Members Faster Than Any Denomination." *CRUX Now*, May 12, 2015. https://cruxnow.com/church/2015/05/12/pew-survey-percentage -of-us-catholics-drops-and-catholicism-is-losing-members-faster -than-any-denomination/.

Quote taken from:

Hugo Rahner, S.J. *The Church, God's Strength in Human Weakness in the Church: Readings in Theology.* New York: P. J. Kennedy and Sons, 1963.

ABSOLUTE MYSTERY

Jack Gilbert quote from:

"The Forgotten Dialect of the Heart." In *Collected Poems.* New York: Knopf, 2012.

Quote from Saint Augustine:

Augustine of Hippo, *Sermon 117:5* (on John 1:1). Original text: *"Si enim comprehendis, non est Deus."*

THE HEART IS A FIRST-CLASS RELIC

Information on the theft of Brother Andre's Heart:

"Brother Andre's Heart." Time.com, May 21, 1973.

"Tipster Sends Police Team to Find Brother Andre's Heart." *The Montreal Gazette*, December 23, 1974.

Information on preserved French hearts:

"Fully Dressed and Preserved 350-Year-Old Corpse of French Noblewoman Found." *The Guardian*, June 3, 2015.

"400-Year-Old Embalmed Hearts Discovered Under French Convent." LiveScience, December 4, 2015. http://www.livescience.com/52985 -embalmed-hearts-discovered-french-convent.html.

Sources

FEAST OF CORPUS CHRISTI

Martin Luther quote from Weimar edition of Martin Luther's works:
D. *Martin Luthers Werke: kritische Gesammtausgabe. Tischreden (Table Talk).* Weimar: H. Böhlaus, 1912.
Quote on the Anglican position on eucharistic adoration comes from:
The Book of Common Prayer. London: Everyman's Library, 1999. New edition of 1662 edition.

ALTAR GIRL

Quotes taken from the following:
Bishop Matthew Clark. *The Fire in the Thornbush.* Pastoral Letter, 1982. http://www.dor.org/index.cfm/linkservid/30beb458-9b4d-c1fd-85c42ed634889d2a/showMeta/0/.
"Cardinal Raymond Burke: Feminized Church and Altar Girls Caused Priest Shortage." Religion News Service, January 7, 2015. http://religionnews.com/2015/01/07/cardinal-raymond-burke-feminized-church-altar-girls-caused-priest-shortage/.
"San Francisco Priest Bars Altar Girls." *Sojourners,* January 28, 2015. https://sojo.net/articles/san-francisco-priest-bars-altar-girls-sparks-another-controversy.
"Pope Francis Says Women Will Never Be Priests." *The Guardian,* November 1, 2016. https://www.theguardian.com/world/2016/nov/01/pope-francis-women-never-roman-catholic-priests-church.
"Bishop's Firing Makes Pope's Priorities Clear." *National Catholic Reporter,* May 4, 2011. https://www.ncronline.org/news/vatican/bishops-firing-makes-popes-priorities-clear.
Pope John Paul II. "Ordinatio Sacerdotalis." 1994. https://w2.vatican.va/content/john-paul-ii/en/apost_letters/1994/documents/hf_jp-ii_apl_19940522_ordinatio-sacerdotalis.html.

MIRACLE OF THE EYES

Quotes and information on the occurrence from the following sources:
"I Saw Little Birds Flying in and out of Mary's Crown": When Irish Statues Moved, and the World Came to Stare. thejournalie.com, July 2015. http://www.thejournal.ie/ballinspittle-moving-statues-2230433-Jul2015/.
"Explaining the Moving Statues Phenomenon, 1985." RTÉ Archives, 2015. https://www.rte.ie/archives/2015/0922/729530-moving-statues-phenomenon/.

Sources

"Statues, Moving." Entry at Encylopedia.com. https://www.encyclopedia
.com/science/encyclopedias-almanacs-transcripts-and-maps/statues
-moving.

Quotes from witnesses found in:

Brian Nugent. *Marian Apparitions in Ireland: and Related Phenomena.*
Morrisville NC: Lulu.com, 2015.

DEVIL'S ADVOCATE

Information on fire, firsthand description, and causes came from the
following articles in the Rochester *Democrat and Chronicle*:

"Nun's Death in Fire Stuns City Parish," February 21, 1967.

"Nun Dies, Priest Burned as Fire Destroys Church," February 21 1967.

"Boy Charged in Setting 4 Church Fires," March 8, 1967.

"50 Years Ago: St. Philip Neri Church Burns, Two Die," February 20, 2017.

ACT OF CONTRITION

James Joyce. *A Portrait of the Artist as a Young Man.* Mineola NY: Dover,
1994. Originally published 1916.

Statistics on frequency of confessions were taken from 2016 data from the
Center for Applied Research in the Apostolate (CARA) at Georgetown
University, Washington DC.

HOLY WATER

Data on percentage of water in organs were taken from:

Mitchell, Hamilton, Steggerda, and Bean. "The Chemical Composition
of the Adult Human Body and Its Bearing on the Biochemistry of
Growth." *The Journal of Biological Chemistry*, February 1945. http://
www.jbc.org/content/158/3/625.full.pdf.

Quoted Bible Passage: Leviticus 14:3–7.

A BRIEF HISTORY OF PRAYER

Flannery O'Connor. *A Prayer Journal.* New York: Farrar, Straus and Giroux, 2013.

Wendell Berry. *Jayber Crow.* Washington DC: Counterpoint Press, 2001.

Thérèse of Lisieux. *The Story of a Soul.* Charlotte NC: TAN Books, 2010.

Abraham Joshua Heschel. *Moral Grandeur and Spiritual Audacity: Essays.*
New York: Farrar, Straus and Giroux, 1997.

Simone Weil. *Gravity & Grace.* New York: Routledge & Kegan Paul, 1952.

Sources

Simone Weil. *Waiting for God*. New York: Routledge & Kegan Paul, 1951.
Information on Wright Brothers found in:
   "Higher, Orville, Higher." *General Aviation News*, August 2015. https://generalaviationnews.com/2015/08/17/higher-orville-higher/.
   The Wright Brothers Website and Historical Timeline, January 2019 http://thewrightbrothersusa.com/one-of-worlds-greatest-stories /wright-brothers-historical-timeline.
John Chrysostom quote found in:
   Edward M. Bounds. *Purpose in Prayer*. New York: Fleming H. Revell Co., 1920.

IN THE AMERICAN LIVES SERIES

The Pat Boone Fan Club: My Life as a White Anglo-Saxon Jew
by Sue William Silverman

Scraping By in the Big Eighties
by Natalia Rachel Singer

In the Shadow of Memory
by Floyd Skloot

Secret Frequencies: A New York Education
by John Skoyles

The Days Are Gods
by Liz Stephens

Phantom Limb
by Janet Sternburg

When We Were Ghouls: A Memoir of Ghost Stories
by Amy E. Wallen

Yellowstone Autumn: A Season of Discovery in a Wondrous Land
by W. D. Wetherell

This Fish Is Fowl: Essays of Being
by Xu Xi

To order or obtain more information on these or other University of Nebraska Press titles, visit nebraskapress.unl.edu.